ALSO BY STANLEY KELEMAN

Bonding (1986)
Emotional Anatomy (1985)
In Defense of Heterosexuality (1982)
Somatic Reality (1979)
Your Body Speaks Its Mind (1975)
Living Your Dying (1974)
Human Ground/Sexuality, Self and Survival (1973)
Todtmoos: A Book of Poems (1971)

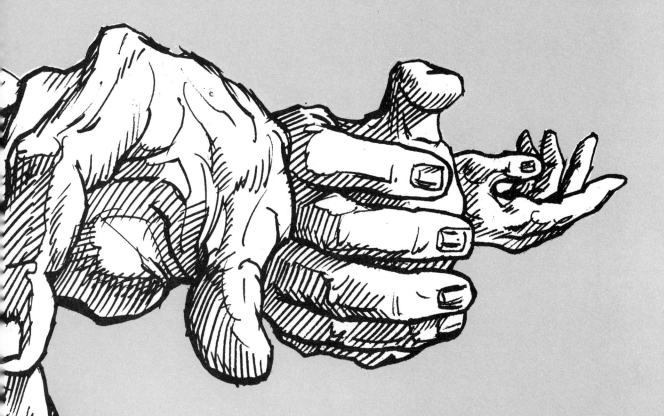

embodying experience

forming a personal life

Stanley Keleman

Center Press, Berkeley

Published by Center Press
2045 Francisco Street
Berkeley, California 94709

Library of Congress Catalogue Number: 86-072980
ISBN 0-934320-12-8

Designed by Randall Goodall

To my daughters, Leah and Katharine

contents

Acknowledgments

To Gene Hendrix, Ph.D., who organized the material,
was general editor, and whose services were invaluable.

To Vincent Perez, the illustrator and artist.

The body forms itself in anticipation
of the aim it serves, it assumes a shape;
a shape for doing work, for fighting, for feeling,
as well as a shape for loving.
> Victor E. Von Gebsattel,
> in *Monatschrift fur
> Psychiatrie und Neurologie,*
> 1932, band 82 p. 113.

Every non-pathological mind seeks in some degree to order and unify experience. This is the expression at the mental level in man of the self-regulating, coordinating, and formative processes of the organism. The genius of mankind, the universal in the individual, expressed in all great religion, art, and science, is the process which transcends the characteristics of the individual scarred by experience and follows the most direct path towards a unified coordination. The universal is that part of the unified truth which is timely.
> L.L. Whyte
> *The Universe of Experience*

introduction

THE LOSS of somatic reality is a current existential dilemma. We are exhorted to "be ourself," "develop ourself," "be true to ourself." Many of us, however, have no felt experience of what is meant by these phrases. Either we live through images, trying to transfer mental experiences to the rest of ourselves, or we try to enliven or intensify experience through chemical substances, social involvement, meditative withdrawal, or physical fitness. Self-knowing may increase but not necessarily somatic understanding.

When emotionally upset we often seek a motive or historical explanation for our behavior or the actions of others. Conflict is usually analyzed in terms of causality: Who started the fight? What were the circumstances or issues? But one could also ask, how did I use myself to engage in that fight? Was my voice demanding or my stance aggressive? Did I tighten belligerently or shrink in rejection? The answers to these questions expose the somatic and emotional nature of behavior and reveal how words, emotions, thoughts and muscular gestures are connected.

Generally our problems continue because we do not know how to organize or disorganize them. We do not know how to disorganize and reform inner psycho-emotional links within ourselves or with others. We may be excited and filled with feelings, but unable to act on it. Or we can act but not inhibit ourselves. We might become angry but not able to stop. We may have ideas and emotions that we cannot join or separate. We may be unable to form emotional experience to bring satisfaction. This inability to use ourself properly often leads to illness or emotional distress.

Each of us has a choice, to continue to identify with old patterns or to reorganize. We can live intensely and grow emotionally or we can live a life that never changes. If we feel the connections that go from inside our bodies to the outside world, and from the surface to the depths, we can re-experience the emotional, bodily depth of our daily life.

Psychological insight is necessary, but of itself does not create change. Current psychology often emphasizes insight and seeks either to uncover the instinctual man underneath the social given, or to overcome the past. When we fail to understand our history as somatic organizations we continue to repeat it. Emotional history, however, is a somatic organization which requires destructuring as well as reorganization. Disorganization by itself can lead to instinctual domination or social imitation, and reorganization is insufficient if it is based solely on the somatic or psychological ideal of some authority.

This book is about the life of the body, the role of the emotions, and man's search for meaning. It suggests how to disassemble outmoded behavior, assemble the elements of experience into new behavior, and how to use yourself to influence personal destiny. It presents the steps of HOW you organize yourself and your life, what is involved, and the language or inner dialogue that sheds light on individual process.

This organizing and formative process is seen throughout nature. Organization brings events together to form; there is an urge in all things animate to take form. Either we perpetuate a form that served us in the past, however painful it may be in the present, or we seek to form what wells up from within.

The anatomical and emotional foundation of this book is found in a companion book, *Emotional Anatomy*, which reveals the blueprint of somatic reality and its meaning in the biological, psychological, and sociological realms. *Embodying Experience* reveals the link between process and form, form and feeling, feeling and function. Process urges us toward differentiation. The organization of experience links the three layers of existence—the animal, the social, and the personal. The subject of this book is how to work with these layers. Together these two books establish the foundation for a modern somatic-emotional education.

1 the nature of the organizing process

EVERY ACTIVITY involves movement, and every movement, however gross or subtle, has an organizing process. This organizing process is based on the biological law that muscles contract and that contraction is followed by elongation. Muscle action has a tidal function. Muscle is not in a state of perpetual spasm or a constant state of relaxation. Muscle elongates and contracts; it expands and shrinks. This rhythm of expansion can be either small or all-encompassing, a micro-tide or a macro-tide of different muscle states called tonus. In the continuum of muscular movement, there is sometimes more tension, sometimes less. The tide alters but never stops. There is sometimes more tension, sometimes less. All activity, even inhibition, involves this organizing process of movement. An understanding of the organizing process is essential in learning how to do things differently because muscle tonus can be altered by the neural centers of the synaptic junction of the spinal cord, or through higher brain synaptic junctions.

All sensations, all emotions, all thoughts are, in fact, organized patterns of motion. By altering basic muscular pulsatory waves, people manipulate their emotions or develop physical stress patterns.

A variety of psycho-physical methodologies recognize the existence of the organizing process and invoke it in their techniques: massage and deep pressure, active physical exericses—running and swimming, the arts of dance and movement, meditation, the bioenergetic approach to muscle tension release, and the re-educative techniques of F.M. Alexander and Edmund Jacobson.

THE ORGANIZING PRINCIPLE

Central to all life is this innate fundamental property, the organizing impulse. All life seeks to make order, to recapitulate an order. This is seen in the genetic code and in the order of nature. Order and organization are synonymous with an inner urge or command that organizes behavior.

Life, at the microcosmic cellular level and the macrocosmic societal and individual organismic level, makes order. Order-making is inherent in every cell. From this order-making, sense and meaning arise. One aggregate of cells talks to another. One part sends messages about its activity to be integrated with other aggregates of activity. This dialogue is elaborated by the flux of signals that come from our senses, feelings, and the action we undertake.

Our deepest identity is concerned with how we organize. Individuality is not an idea, what somebody tells us about who we are, or a social artifact. It is the recognition of how we do things, a sense of order that is established by our own life process. This natural process can be the foundation of our personal lives and provide an immediate, vital, and vivid sense of who we are.

Order is not a command, "make order." Rather, it is the way a person does something, takes in experience, digests it, and acts on it. Order is a sense deep in the unconscious, felt but not quite articulated. When something is not in order or disorganized, one senses it and seeks to make order.

Once felt, order and organization become the foundation for personal identity and are not easily destroyed. When a person's natural order is interrupted, a whole series of reactions is evoked—annoyance, sadness, helplessness, and anger.

The rules and rhythms of nature have always organized human affairs. The experience of the organizing impulse gives knowledge and insight into the difference between being lived and volitional living, between fate and choice.

THE ACCORDION

The image of an accordion illustrates the organizing process. Both function through building and releasing tension and pressure. These different states of tension and pressure form the language of ourselves. For example, the heart beats at a rate that varies with increases or decreses of pressure. This expansion and contraction is diastole and systole. The heart speeds up when we are afraid, and slows down when we sleep.

Spontaneous and natural actions, like the beating heart or the sucking of a nursing infant, are patterns of organized movements. "Hold still," "be good," "keep quiet" are instructions we consciously organize into specific somatic patterns.

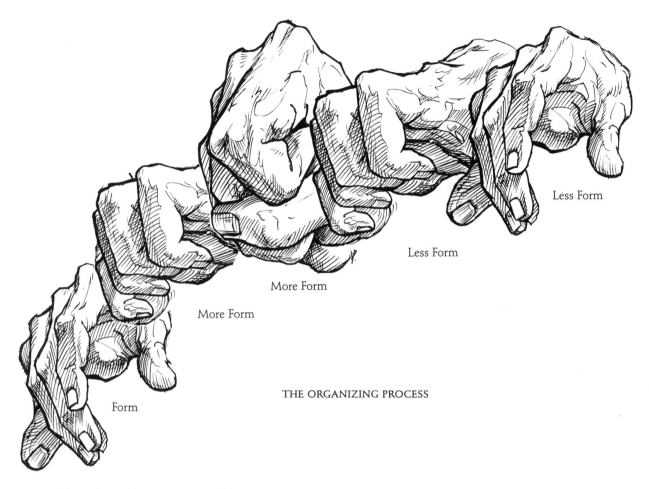

Form

More Form

More Form

Less Form

Less Form

THE ORGANIZING PROCESS

Many of these learned organizations foster maturity, yet others cause conflict or pain. "I want to reach out for contact but I have to hold still" is an example.

This principle—bodily tensions result from interferences in rhythmic contraction and release—serves as the foundation of somatic process therapy whose goal is to re-establish patterns of elongation and contraction. Using a technique based on the image of an accordion, I ask clients to intensify and tighten a pattern of behavior and then let it go slowly in increments. I deliberately do not ask them to let go at the beginning, but to tighten up first and then let it go in order to restore the pattern's flow.

This accordion procedure teaches how emotions are inhibited and expressed, how thoughts become action, how sense is made and meaning formed. The principle of the accordion involves discrete stages and a specific procedure. It means more than just tightening and releasing the musculature. Feeling, image, arousal, and inhibition—all are involved. The procedure for discovering one's organizing process is called the HOW methodology.

THE PULSATORY CONTINUUM

To the Inside, Away from the World
Contraction

To the World, Away from the Inside
Expansion

To and from the World
To and from the Inside

Several years ago I developed a left-sided sciatic pain that became progressively worse and resisted all sorts of treatments. I finally discovered that getting in and out of my small car required an unstable maneuver that placed all my weight on one leg. To hold my weight in this position caused a muscle spasm which resulted in the sciatic pain. To overcome the pattern, I had to stop this maneuver whenever I got in or out of my car. Learning how to stop it, how not to repeat the same action automatically, brought me face to face with what I was unknowingly doing.

How could I use myself to get in and out of the car with more stability? I would need to keep my weight more equally distributed, to swivel my hips, and to stand up without banging my head on the car roof. By taking time to learn what I was doing, I stopped reflex action. First, I visualized my legs and feet performing my usual swivel. Then I tried to feel myself doing it, paying attention that my image, perception, and action were coordinated. I stopped using my car for a little while and waited for the old spasticity to relax. Once my contractions softened and I no longer felt pain in my hip, I had a chance to suggest new action pathways, practice them, and feel my new muscle pattern. Learning how I used myself muscularly, sensorily, imaginatively, emotionally, gave me a dynamic insight into how a body gets distorted in emotional situations and how different patterns could occur.

We all have complex organized patterns of action and expression. Anger, for example, has programmed patterns of crying, shouting or hitting. We use some patterns of action to suppress, hide, or inhibit our responses. We practice how to stop crying or work to control our tempers. We all struggle to control or hide socially disapproved behaviors and to master approved ones. We do this by trying to get a picture or an idea of what is wanted, and then use our muscles to carry out the action.

As a child, how many times was I told not to cry? If I was about to cry, I knew I could stop by biting my lip. So I recalled the movement of biting my lip and re-enacted doing it. I then practiced the movement until I didn't have to bite my lip, I could keep from crying by clenching my jaw. As an adult, I control my tears by repeating this pattern. When I ask myself how I prevent crying or expressing tenderness I say, "I just do it." If I persist in asking specifically how I do this, I might discover, "I grab my chest muscles" or "I see myself as strong and tall and I try to be tall and get the feeling of being strong." I tighten my stomach muscles, stiffen my neck, clench my jaw, and if I feel I am still going to cry, I'll do these things more intensely, until I become one giant spasm.

We all do this, consciously or unconsciously, step by step. We contract muscles, and more muscles, until we master the pattern that wishes to emerge. Although we finally create an image and feeling of emotional strength, spasticity becomes the basis of a self-image and an accompanying thought pattern "I am strong."

Helping people identify patterns of self-use is the primary agenda in somatic process work. Learning how to end a pattern is the second step. Before a pattern can be changed it is necessary to experience how the pattern happens. The brain can be trained to recognize different patterns of tension in a continuum of action.

For example, when someone is angry he may clench his fists. If he tries clenching his fists lightly he will probably not feel a sense of anger. But clenching tightly he will recognize the angry feeling. If he completes the action of clenching his fists tightly, he can then tense less and less. He learns how it feels to open and close his fists in varying stages, and practices, through intensifying, to become less intense. With this recognition, he learns to give up fist-clenching as a pattern of anger and to substitute a new pattern, such as a verbal phrase, "I am angry," or "don't do that."

There is a muscular sequence to activites like mouth-clenching or lip-biting. It is a continuum of increasing and decreasing muscle contraction that is the process of emotional and behavioral control. It is the way to form behavior and to create new forms.

WHAT THE HOW IS

The HOW exercise brings you to the point of experiencing how you do a particular activity—how you go from forming an image of something to actually doing it. The procedure is to simpy ask yourself, "How am I doing such and such?" For example, "How am I reading this book?" In asking this question, you find numerous possible answers. "I am sitting on a chair. I am holding my neck stiff. I am reading with an attitude of expectation or skepticism. When I am like this I hold my breath. I feel suspended. I won't permit myself to get too excited."

The HOW exercise helps you know yourself, helps you develop an awareness of the patterns of sensation and motor-emotional rhythms that your brain must know to integrate new behavior. The HOW exercise makes explicit the way you use yourself in any given situation. After learning the basic procedure, you can use it in other situations. You can call up memories of old actions and the accompanying muscular contractions, see how you are doing what you would rather not do, and develop new ways to use yourself in the future.

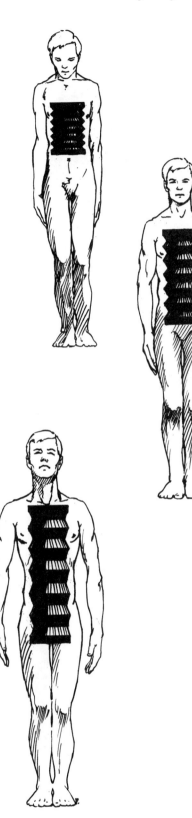

THE CONTINUUM FROM SELF-GATHERING TO SELF-EXTENDING

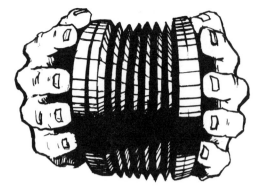

Contraction

Expansion

THE EXPANSION-CONTRACTION ACCORDION

The HOW process has five recognizable steps, identified by these questions:

step one
WHAT AM I DOING?

step two
HOW AM I DOING IT?

step three
HOW DO I STOP DOING IT?

step four
WHAT HAPPENS WHEN I STOP DOING IT?

step five
HOW DO I USE WHAT I HAVE LEARNED?

To use the HOW process and the accordion exercise—intensifying and relaxing muscular contractions—involves several steps. First, there are pictures in the form of images or ideas, or patterns of feeling of what you think is proper action. "I see myself as strong." "I feel strong." Or a picture might emerge from what others say. Next, very concrete actions carry out these images as social poses. For example, the neck and spine muscles stiffen to show pride and determination or the abdomen pulls in to show self-control.

If these patterns of contraction or stress become painful, you try to find relief—take hot baths, use drugs or alcohol, have massages, try to act in a countervailing way. Many people, for example, try to end the tensions of exaggerated pride by acting humble. Some people realize how contracted they are and spontaneously let go of their muscle spasms. When you stop, inhibit, relax long-standing patterns of action that have become automatic and deeply ingrained, you experience deep somatic upwellings of sensations and feelings—powerful currents of response which are not verbal. This is called "ah-ha," or insight, or intuition. These responses are profound internal events representing another stage of self-organization.

From this point of intuition there are choices to be made. You have something you didn't have before—insight, feeling, action, new experience. You can stop at this place believing that such experiences alone make you different. Or you can forget what occurred, or try to put this learning into operation all at once and end up overwhelmed and inadequate. You could stay in the place of insight, hoping for more. You might deny and dismiss your experience. Or you can build a discipline of practicing the step-by-step lessons you have learned and begin to create a new form. The final step is your response—what you do with the previous four steps.

STEP ONE
Surface
Image
Story
Situation
Structure

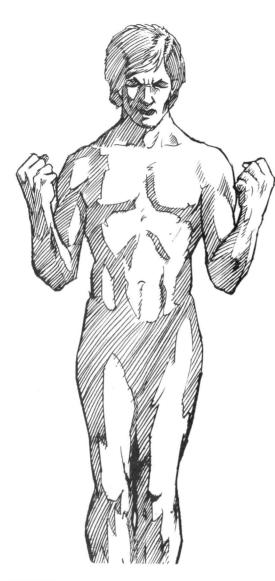

STEP TWO
   Organization:
   Creating a Second Layer of Experience

                    STEP THREE
                       Disorganization:
                       Creating a Third Layer of Experience

To practice the HOW methodology, in Step One, make a picture or image of yourself, how you think about or imagine yourself in a particular situation. In Step Two, discover the muscle pattern with which you organize this image. For example, "I tighten my neck to be proud." In Step Three, experience destructuring the muscular pattern of contraction, such as the stiff neck. In Step Four, stay with your experience and see how new insights, feelings, and emotions well up. And, finally, in Step Five, look for your response to all of this. Is your tendency to practice new behavior, dismiss the experience, or look for more insight?

The HOW exercise, therefore, involves a series of process questions:

step one

WHAT IS MY IMAGE OF MYSELF IN MY PRESENT SITUATION?

step two

HOW DO I MUSCULARLY CREATE THIS IMAGE
AND PERPETUATE IT?

step three

HOW DO I END THE WAY I HAVE EMBODIED MYSELF?

step four

WHAT HAPPENS TO ME WHEN I END THIS?

step five

WHAT RESPONSE DO I MAKE TO THIS?

THE HOW STEPS IN ACTION

STEP ONE: THE IMAGE OF MY PRESENT SITUATION

I am waiting. I form an image of the situation, I conceive a shape. I say to myself that this situation is temporary. I make a picture of "letting time go by" or "keeping myself entertained." I watch events move toward a certain expected finish.

STEP TWO: HOW I USE MYSELF

By intensifying my muscular posture, I feel the way I use myself. Muscular contractions are the dialogue that makes the image of intentions. So I ask, how do I maintain my patience, by "taking it easy," or "chomping at the bit"? Perhaps by walking more slowly or taking smaller steps or holding myself rigid to suppress impatience. I may squeeze my chest to control breathing or hold myself like a ramrod, locking my knees, compressing personal space, squeezing inner organs in order to be patient. These bodily postures are somatic images, capable of being consciously experienced.

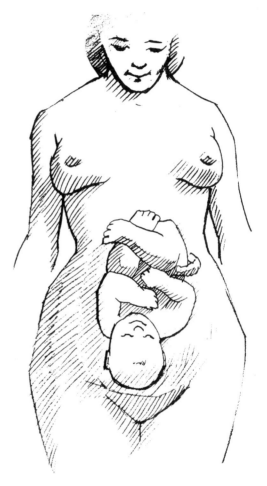

STEP FOUR
Creation
Depths
Pause
Incubation
Gestation

STEP THREE: HOW I DISORGANIZE OR END STRUCTURES
THAT I NO LONGER NEED

Use the accordion exercise. By intensifying a pattern of
tension, such as the squeezed chest or the locked knees, and
taking it to its extreme, I can then back off, let up, relax a
bit, release the spasms, and experience the feeling of muscle
elongation. This process ends organized spasm. As form
disorganizes its intensity, it is like a fever breaking. Tightening more, more, still more, then letting it go a bit, a little bit
more, still more, gives the sense of the accordion-like process
of tighter, loose, looser, giving form, more form, less form.

STEP FOUR: INCUBATION, CREATION

The dialogue of neural orders, visual and emotional memories and muscular action slowly creates a silence. It is, in
many ways, an incubation. In this pause I find a natural
whirlpool of excitement, a deafening silence of feeling, or
an upwelling of electric currents that warm and melt. The
hormones of the brain arouse images of new experience
accompanied by memories of the past. I may create memories of being a child waiting for my mother at the bus stop
and the feeling that this waiting was forever. Then I remember her coming back. Or I may have a feeling that informs
me I can wait without holding my back rigid. I can experience myself in an entirely original way. My anxious pattern
of waiting can be destructured and a unique waiting take its
place.

STEP FIVE: USING WHAT I HAVE LEARNED

At this point there is choice. I can forget what I have
experienced and go back to the old way. I can repeat the five
steps but get enamored at one step. I can wait endlessly for
more insight or feeling. Or I can use what I have learned
and form a new response. To do this I practice using myself
in a new way, turning insight into action. I consistently give
commands to myself to use my eyes, muscles, feet differently. I remind myself to loosen the constrictions of my
chest, unlock my tight knees and breathe more fully. This is
how my inner world finds a way to the outer world, my
inner knowing becomes social action. This is a linking of
brain, heart, muscle. The key to this step is practice, again
and again in different ways, to form new response.

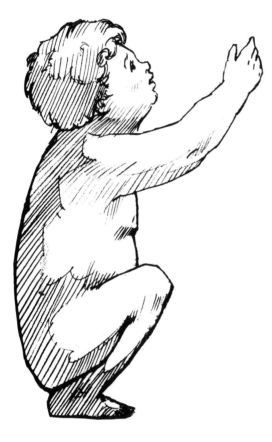

STEP FIVE
Return to the Surface:
Reorganization or New Form

daily life

DAILY LIVING involves creating different somatic shapes to deal with a variety of changing external circumstances. The day starts with ending sleep and concludes with ending wakefulness. The succession of events inbetween includes interactions with family, neighbors, work associates, fellow commuters, and so forth. Leaving family in a warm and loving mood. How? Entering the daily rush to work. How? Leaving the traffic jam and entering work. How? The boss and you have a disagreement. You feel inadequate. How do you construct inadequacy? How could you form a different response? As work ends, you rejoin the commuter rush. How? Again entering your home and family, you are a different form in that situation. How? Your wife and you have a disagreement and you feel guilty. How?

The events of daily living provide the arena, while the HOW exercise provides the tool to explore personal process. Instead of talking to yourself subvocally, examining, blaming, or finding fault, use the HOW to let your form speak to you, teaching from the inside how a response is shaped to an external event. How is an event taken inside? What do you shape as a response? If your habitual response is self-defeating, how do you end it, let another response form, until it becomes a new form?

STEPS TWO AND THREE:
ORGANIZING AND DISORGANIZING
  Organization of Form
  Disorganization of Form

STEP ONE: PICTURING A PRESENT SITUATION

Be alert to yourself in the present situation. Look in a mirror and see your body form. For example, chest up, stiff neck. Ask yourself, "How do I do this?" or "How do I make this form?"

STEP TWO: HOW YOU DO IT

Note how your muscles give a sense of your bodily-emotional form. Try to perceive yourself through all your feelings, senses and thought forms. Ask yourself, "How do I maintain my form, my image? "How do I do this somatically?" Your answers may be observations like "I pull up my chest," "I suck up my abdomen in order to think," or "I let my belly muscles collapse." What is the inner dialogue necessary to recognize that your shoulders are uplifted or your brain is squeezed? Attempts to recall your somatic pattern will not work. If you catch yourself trying to recall, use your muscles to contract and let go, to actually feel and sense what you do.

In this way your idea of yourself extends into the bodily realm: "I know how I lift my shoulders by lifting them," "I know how to let them down by dropping them bit my bit." The question then becomes "What signals my muscles to go up or down?" or "What are the images and ideas that are part of my continuum of contraction?"

Answering these questions, you learn how to talk to yourself somatically. Do not expect a straight line of thinking, or even answers recognizable by words or concepts. Your answers may be feelings and images. Contact with yourself may disappear. This is the way of process. What you are learning is part of a chain of events meant to facilitate forming.

STEP THREE: HOW YOU DESTRUCTURE YOUR SOMATIC IMAGE

Destructuring includes all the ways to stop doing something. It may require a relaxation response or its opposite, a focus on release if you find yourself squeezed or vice versa. Use the learning of Step Two, your pattern, and add to it the accordion procedure of muscle intensification and lessening. If you found that you sucked up your belly, you can use the feeling of sucking up to end it. Suck up hard, do it less, do it more, do it less, until you have the feeling of letting your abdomen down. You train yourself in the feeling of ending. Look for the feeling that something is coming down, that you are coming down, giving up something.

Ask yourself, "How do I separate from my rituals and stereotypes of behavior?" Disorganizing your stereotypes may trigger a deep fear of losing control, becoming disorganized, losing a sense of order and reality. Ask yourself, "How do I maintain order?" "How do I tighten to do this?" "How much do I dare disorganize?" "How will I respond?" Here ordinary understanding ends. Through the accordion exercise you end rituals. Now, with customary responses inhibited, the brain is flooded with the sensations of activity. Time stands still or speeds up; your universe may take on strange forms.

STEP FOUR: HOW YOU INCUBATE EMOTIONALLY

Step Four is an open state, a pause mode. You actively wait for new response. This waiting is neither passive nor meditative. It is being alert without watching yourself. It is like expecting a visitor. This visitor may come as a feeling, an intuition, an image, or an association. Waiting is creation, gestation, incubation. It is a pause in which you feel elements of something about to happen. The attitude of openness is one of containment, something being held yet not squeezed. There is a sense of filling up.

Images, feeling, sensations and ideas well up. This is a peaceful place. You have an inner sense that a direction is going to come. You are between what has ended and what has not yet arrived, in a pregnant place.

While in this open state try to prevent immediate involuntary muscular changes. The question to ask is, "How am I waiting?" or "How is my open state interrupted or prolonged?" Is it interrupted by thoughts, urges to action, or anxiety? Is it elongated by deadening excitement? Do you pace? Or daydream obsessively? When new impulses or excitement or images come, do you respond in the old ways? Are responses prematurely formed into an action? Keep open until your pause state begins to mature and grow itself.

Eventually, something occurs. There is a gathering together —a new image, a feeling, a dream, a way of doing something. There is a response.

> *To embody your experience*
> *is to transcend*
> *your somatic-emotional history.*

STEP FIVE: RESPONSE, THE PRACTICE OF FORMING

Choose your response to what has occurred in the preceding step. You might dismiss what has occurred, forget about it, seek solace by remaining at one of the earlier steps, or begin to create a new form through practice.

What is forming? How do you make incarnate feeling and thought? How do you take cognitive hold and then put into effect what you have come to know? The forming process is the most consciously creative part of your existence. At this point you apply what you have learned about self-organization. You can experiment with bringing muscles into play through feeling, vision, old rituals, or imitation. This process involves more than conscious control. To integrate emotions, cognition, and muscles, the unprogrammed and the learned program must merge. By applying conscious participation to unconscious happenings, you create new forms to which you then try to be faithful. It takes a lot of practice.

DAILY LIFE: PROBLEM SOLVING AND CONFLICT RESOLUTION

Life is problem solving, organizing to deal with the challenges and conflicts of existence. Human nature has a highly differentiated system for tolerating ambiguities, unresolved situations, and for behaviors that do not have a common pathway. The HOW process is a way to conceive a situation and organize a response. It gives a way to inhibit habitual responses, a way to bide your time . . . wait . . . pause . . . divert yourself . . . reconceive the situation . . . and then reorganize it.

The basic five steps of the HOW can be applied to any problem:

SELF-REFLECTION EXERCISE
PROBLEM-SOLVING

1. How do I imagine the problem? (Do I blame myself, blame others, look for causes, seek solutions)

2. How do I somatically organize to deal with the problem? How do I hold my shoulders, eyes, jaw, muscles?

3. How do I step back to separate, dissociate, disorganize the way I deal with the problem?

4. How do I permit new images and insights and plans to incubate and then emerge?

5. How do I take what has occurred and either use myself differently to reform the problem and myself or remain in the same stance?

INTERNAL CONFLICT

Conflict is a dynamic tension between contradictory aspects of a situation. We often experience contradictions between intent and direction. Various layers compete with one another—to delay gratification, to inhibit security demands, to sublimate desire. There may be conflict between moving towards the world or inward into one's self. The wish to approach another may be simultaneously inhibited by fear or shame. The brain perceives danger, the heartbeat speeds up in preparation for flight, yet the surface muscles resist.

SELF-REFLECTION EXERCISE
INTERNAL CONFLICT

1. How do I experience internal conflict? (Do I have a picture, a feeling, two feelings at war with each other?)

2. What is my body posture? Is it a twist or a facing forward followed by a feeling of turning away? How do I tense my muscles to sustain this?

3. How, through increasing and decreasing this pattern, can I inhibit, cease, withdraw from, or deprogram this pattern?

4. How do I remain unorganized, without apparent form? How is the conflict now encapsulated?

5. How do I facilitate another action pattern to resolve or contain my previous one, or do I return to it?

EXTERNAL CONFLICT

Conflict is not only internal. It is often outside ourselves, in relations with family members, employers, friends, fellow workers. The HOW procedure converts these conflicts into a way to know yourself. When you learn to organize or disorganize conflict situations, you can abandon stereotyped responses.

In the HOW process it is not important who is right and who is wrong. The concern is only how you organize the situation, how you can disorganize it, and how you can re-organize it differently.

SELF-REFLECTION EXERCISE
EXTERNAL CONFLICT

1. What is my present conflict? What are the roles I take? How do I embody the situation? (Shrink, inflate, turn away, accommodate)

2. How am I playing my part, facilitating it? What are the automatic actions I do to maintain my role in the situation?

3. How will I inhibit my part? How will I make separations and distinctions? What muscles do I let go? What do I stop thinking or doing?

4. How will I contain myself until there is a reference from inside to work from? How will I not go back to my old pattern while waiting for a new image or organization to emerge?

5. How do I facilitate a new way of behaving?

*To have form
is to be alive.
But to remain fixed
in a form
is to stagnate.
Our destiny is to
continue to form.*

Say you have difficulty with your spouse. You believe things cannot stay the way they are. In Step One you discover that you deal with this conflict through anger and hostility. Step Two gives the physical experience of your anger and hostility. Step Three is how you disorganize anger. If you are organized to be combative, Step Three involves deprogramming the fight stance. By lowering your center of gravity, you no longer view the situation as an insult. You have a chance to relate differently, to de-stress. You accept the situation, but deprogram the fight-flight mechanism— batten down, wait it out, take it in and keep making modifications. You contain it. You keep shaping the situation.

At work you may be cooperative yet seek recognition. You want security but also to be challenged. In addition, you want response from others. These needs may create conflict with others or within yourself. One part of your body holds back another part, that is, you keep your mouth shut in order not to offend anyone. You make yourself submissive to authorities by deflating your chest. Alternately, you make yourself bigger when you want to exert your authority. Use the HOW procedure to experience and reorganize work problems and conflict.

THE CASE OF MORRIS

Morris is a middle-aged man who has worked for other people or organizations all his life. Now he is in business for himself. He is accustomed to taking action quickly but now faces the uncertainties of contract negotiations and working with many organizations rather than just one. In the following description, Morris talks about his use of the HOW process to handle a conflict in his work situation. He has to wait before he can act and this causes him difficulty.

MORRIS

This year is going to involve changes in my work life. The industry I work for is undergoing financial upheaval, and the pattern of my work is thus undergoing change. My stance towards this involves waiting, Step One: How do I wait? At the conceptual level, I talk to myself and tell myself that things are going to be okay. As I wait and talk to myself I freeze the upper third of my body in a series of complex maneuvers that seem to have no starting point. Step Two: My tongue presses strongly against my palate and I tense my neck up into my brain. I harden my upper back, collapse the front of my chest, pull in with my ribs, under my arms; even my neck is pulled down—as through I were a turtle pulling its head inward. I brace my jaw and the bone structure of my palate. My breathing becomes shallow, and everything from the diaphragm and lower ribs becomes dense, narrowed, still, expectant, held tightly, silent.

As I try to make this more and less, (Step Three), I experience a stance with many subtle variations, one that I am quite familiar with. It seems to be the way that I approach the world and others most of the time. It is a sort of defiance (Step One). How do I organize it (Step Two)? I cock my head backwards, compress my neck and pull it in, while further pressing with my tongue against my palate. At the same time I pull inward with my shoulders and rib cage. As I exaggerate this, (Step Three), I feel the smooth muscles of my tongue and esophagus tighten all the way down into my belly. My inner organs harden and press downward. I compress more and more until I become an internal hardened spasm which gets hot. I shake from the inside out. I can hold this forever. As I release, the decontracting begins in the muscles of the belly and diaphragm, relaxing the esophagus, loosening the chest and armpits, and extending the shoulders. This softens my tongue and slightly moves the crown of my head forward. My palate, brain, and neck soften. After this, I experience a softening internally, a liquid feeling in my eyes, as if tears were coming.

As I play the accordion of more and less with this complex organization, I experience three different phases: one in the belly that compresses and pulls downward, one in the chest that is pulling in and downward, and one in the head-neck-tongue-eyes-palate. Step by step each piece engages the others to make a total gesture. I experience a loose expression on the outside surfaces, making these changes unnoticeable to the world. There is stubbornness in my gesture, and willfulness, but it is an internal state. Yet there is also fear, a watch for something that may startle, surprise, or hurt me. And when I let it go a little bit, I experience a softening, a dampening of the eyes, and sadness. I am sad, but can't show it. I am scared and can't express it. I am mad but must contain it (Step Three).

I meet the present with my past, embodied in this stance. I brace, stiffen, narrow, internally focus, freeze, and wait. The present and the past become one in this form.

After I work with myself, I go out into the world, yet as I carry on my daily business, this experience is still with me. I feel my shoulders going up and my head pulling inward, so make a subtle shift when conversing with a friend (Step Five). I practice reorganizing this stance many times a day and each time capture more subtle aspects. I can destructure my stance of defiance, fear, and waiting, examining each situation for its potential threat or possibility for rejection. It is slow work, but it offers hope.

This case represents a failure to reorganize. Morris uses the steps of the HOW but keeps distancing himself from the internal reorganization of crying or anger.

3 why the how works

ALL HUMAN behavior involves images, feeling, sensation, emotion, and action in a layered process. The HOW steps reveal this layered process and show that what appears to be simple is also complex.

FORMING

Existence has a pattern and seeks a pattern. Every living thing develops, maintains, and changes form. Life is this process of forming. This tendency towards form is universal. In the language of phenomenology, forming is life's absolute imperative.

The basic urge of life is not replication, self-preservation through reproduction. It is not aggression, sexuality, community, or intimacy. The basic urge is toward form, both communal and individual. Without form our identity and relationships suffer. Existence no longer has an organization.

Forming requires organization. Organization is the HOW of the formative process. The laws of organization are not random, they have an order.

Each person's embryological history illustrates the HOW of body making. There is a process which guides the development of two cells initially joined together as they grow into the trillions of cells that form an infant body; that process has definite rules and procedures. I described this is *In Defense of Heterosexuality.*

Forming continues after birth. Growing up from infancy to adulthood involves more than a proliferation of cells. Genetically we are given a body but we also form that body through our experience and the way in which we use ourselves. Man has a brain that continues to grow after birth; experience affects its forming. We are increasingly adaptive as we grow, forming our experience and being formed by it. Daily living gives flesh to our experience. Physical form manifests our invisible experiences.

There are steps and procedures to forming. Certain conditions must be present and others must be established for forming to occur. For example, there must a a certain pH and temperature in the womb for implantation to occur as well as certain elements of nutrition for growth to proceed. Outside the womb, conditions must continue to be favorable with adequate food, shelter, emotional contact.

Societal tradition like genetic tradition transmits experience. Bowel training rituals are an introduction into society's method of learning self-control. In order to master this learning we must use ourselves. Schooling, likewise, is a tradition that creates form, demanding that we master the knowledge of the society.

The forming process integrates and uses all our capacities— imitation, desire, feeling, analysis, imagination, rehearsal, recall, and projection. Through these functions we live our biological, emotional, psychological existence and shape a multidimensional human world.

To understand how you make your life, it is not important to ask about motivation (the why), location (the where), or time (the when). All those things are revealed in the answer to the organizational question "How do I do this?" or "How is this happening?" The Five Steps are exercises in imaginative, emotional and muscular thinking, steeped in the visual, auditory, tactile, kinesthetic, and proprioceptive images of somatic existence.

PULSATION

The most basic action of living is pulsation, a jellyfish-like pumping motion. It is seen in all of the organs, all of the muscles. It gives the organism its ability to alter its own movement.

Imagine a jellyfish propelling itself through the water, squeezing and unsqueezing itself. When fearful or annoyed, it quickens its pulsation, making itself firmer and swimming faster. When it is at ease, the jellyfish spreads out in a circular form, bobbing relaxed on the ocean with few detectable contractile rhythms.

Life process operates on similar rhythmical waves of pulsation, waves that we have the ability to slow down, hold still or speed up. Through inhibition we regulate the amplitude, volume, and rate of the waves of expansion and contraction. In the HOW exercise we use inhibition to heighten arousal, assertion, and their expression in images and feelings that give meaning to existence.

Pulsatory movements help internal circulation and increase internal sensation and feeling. We experience pulsation in the muscles and in the contents of the visceral tubes, heart and blood vessels, and sexual organs. As the nervous system pulsates, it helps to intensify and modulate the hydraulic pressure of swelling and shrinking. Hormonal tides of adrenaline, testosterone, and estrogen contribute to the pulsatory pattern with chemicals that increase or decrease arousal.

The HOW methodology reveals pulsatory patterns, the configuration of thinking, feeling, and action. If pulsatory patterns are weak, boundaries are weak, and we have difficulty making form. We become underformed. Sometimes we compensate by holding, contracting, squeezing to create form. If pulsatory patterns are over-controlled, boundaries are too dense, we are muscle spastic and cannot move freely. We have too much form.

THE ACCORDION AS A PUMP

Like an accordion, the human is a flexible hollow tube with many chambers that are capable of expanding and elongating, shrinking and compacting, squeezing and releasing. The smooth muscles of the hollow intestines and their pouch-like segments move liquids along by waves of swelling and compaction, functioning like an accordion. Skeletal and surface muscles contribute to the accordion pump-like action in a manner similar to a weightlifter curling a barbell. A common phrase among weightlifters is "pumping iron," meaning their muscles lift weight like a pump. Skeletal muscle has this cylinder or pump-like function.

The accordion-like function of skeletal and smooth muscle generates an awareness of motion. The sensations we feel are the imprint of neural activity that makes self-regulation possible. As we move, the changing shapes of the cells create pressure; that increasing and decreasing pressure is central to somatic process. Internally, the jellyfish-like pumping of the brain and the spinal cord bring different areas of the brain into contact with one another to create associations and images. Pressure brings surfaces together. Closeness and contact generate pressure. Love, anger, fear, and feeling in general are related to sensations of pressure.

The HOW process mimics the natural way we function. By emphasizing internal patterns of squeezing, pressure, release we acquire knowledge about excitement, arousal, and feeling. We come to understand that a continuum of pressure and excitement connects and separates us to the world around us as well as to ourselves. This peristalsis of connection-separation, pressure-less pressure regulates the layers by which we organize behavioral responses.

The formative journey means to put one's self into contact with a bigger order.

All living creatures are excitable, capable of being aroused either by themselves or by others. This arousal can be observed in the search for food or mates as well as in the agitated behavior of avoidance or aggression. Arousal has its opposite pole, discharge and motor action. All creatures display this discharge and release. The accumulation of excitement and emotion has to be expressed. This is evident in children's play, in cries of loss and grief, in shrieks and menacing charges when threat is present. It is experienced in lovemaking, and emotional expression. It is further seen in the pacing of trapped animals or the sexual aggression of aroused mammals.

Arousal followed by release is a key process of existence. Cells swell and divide; the heart experiences diastole and systole; the brain fills with ideas and expresses itself in action. People seek stimuli to arouse them to action. We fill up with our own excitement and seek ways to express ourselves. Failing to find a means of expression, we suffer from convulsions or the raw acting out of our frustrations.

The HOW process brings about emotional and excitatory arousal as well as its expression. The first two steps of the HOW process focus attention on ourselves, how we attach to excitement, how we connect to others, how we use our excitement, how we stimulate or inhibit arousal. Step Three frees excitation and emotions through the accordion-like increase and decrease of inhibition. In Step Four deep underground currents rouse the flesh and mind with sensations and hot emotions, vivid desires move toward the exterior and toward form. Grief and sighs of relief are found, as are stormy, unpredictable feelings and anticipatory action. The final step involves our response to this process, a return to our original arousal pattern or learning through practice to form our arousal differently.

Arousal and inhibition are the essential element of self-knowledge. When reflex becomes susceptible to self-management, we end a stimulus-response type existence. We begin to have some say in our self-forming; we learn from experience.

SELF-REFLECTION EXERCISE
AROUSAL

1. How do I picture being aroused or excited? (Out-of-control, restrained, electrified)

2. How do I organize my arousal, sustain it, allow it to swell and reach all parts of myself?

3. How could I increase or decrease my pattern of arousal?

4. In the pause, how does the ground of excitement organize me?

5. How do I use this learning? Do I return to my previous arousal pattern or practice living with greater or lesser excitation?

THE ROLE OF THE BRAIN

The three areas of the brain—cortex, mid-brain, brain stem—contribute to increased awareness. Each is a regulation center able to develop pulsatory wave configurations, and make them shorter and more intense or longer and less intense. Each can produce long, rolling curves of modified arousal; fast, discrete waves of action; of flat curves of hibernation. The lower the complexity of organismic life, the more gross and primitive the waves of motility. The higher the complexity of organismic life the greater the need for coordination and regulation.

The whole range of brain function is involved in the HOW exercise. Through this exercise we instruct the brain through a feedback loop in which the organs of the body and various layers of the brain interact. From the top of the brain, the occipital and temporal lobes, come images and a sense of time. As muscular contractions intensify, the parietal lobes generate muscular images. As muscles intensify and release, the sensory-motor area of the brain responds. The right and left brain engage in a dialogue of differences in muscular activity. Thus the feeling associated with the contractions is revealed. Fear, anger, pleasure are localized in the thalamus and hypothalamus. The cerebellum is involved in the spontaneous adjustment to gravity, upright posture, orientation in the gravitational field. When electric currents start, or the heart begins to race, or there is sexual arousal, we are in the brain stem and spinal cord—those deep regions where we experience creation without words or symbols. As we ascend from the brain stem's innate movements, feelings of pleasure and awe organize the thalamus mid-brain. To find ways to express these feelings as appropriate social gestures, we carry on a dialogue between the cortex, with its ability for muscular differentiation, and the thalamus, with its feeling. These steps of organization are the real language of knowledge about the self.

The brain's main function is to facilitate a sequence of events. The brain organizes stimuli into various layers at various rates through the geometry of its form. The density of fibers in the bottleneck of the brain stem speeds up impulses. The curved structure of the limbic system slows impulses down and turns them on themselves. The pulsating cortex makes new connections by bringing various impulses into association. The brain locates stimuli and knows how to uncover intent. It informs the rest of the organism, but its main concern is how excitation and impulses are going on. The brain is as much a part of the forming process as is the rest of the body.

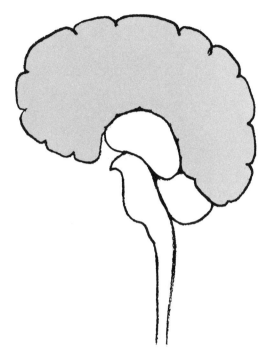

CORTEX
Outer Social Layer
The Societal Brain

The brain pulsates. Its pattern of pulsation or organ motility increases and decreases pressure. Through pressure regulation, motility is regulated to alter metabolism, the movements of coming and going, hormonal activity, even thought patterns. The pulsating brain keeps the ventricle fluids ebbing and flowing, bringing areas of the brain into changing relationships.

THALAMUS-MIDBRAIN
Middle Muscle Layer
The Personal-Emotional
Brain

INHIBITION AND THE BRAIN

The brain is not a switching device that is either on or off. Neither is it a telephone switchboard. The brain is a living ocean of electrohormonal currents generated by the total soma including the brain itself. The flow of these currents traveling over nerves and muscles speeds up and slows down process. When certain internal events slow down, other events emerge.

Muscles, which in some ways are like fat nerves, are waiting, eager to act, and have to be restrained. This restraint is inhibition. The inhibition of certain actions and events permits others to emerge. By inhibiting contraction we may be able to articulate fears, or see where we make mistakes. By inhibiting innate sexual responses, we may be able to increase tenderness or become more aware of it.

Your Body Speaks Its Mind points out that to be yourself, to be in action, diminishes concurrent self-awareness. To be conscious you must slow yourself, inhibit your process. It then becomes possible to know yourself. It is one of life's paradoxes that spontaneity, creativity, and human growth depend upon the ability to be unspontaneous, to inhibit responses. The brain is an organ structured to delay or stop. The function of stopping is to achieve a more differentiated and refined action. It is also meant to prolong a gesture, to perpetuate a connection or relationship so that more learning can occur. Through inhibition, physical skills as well as emotions are developed. Tenderness becomes love, anger becomes compassion, speech becomes song.

THE FUNCTION OF INHIBITION

Inhibition is a form of stopping, of holding, of making steady. Certainly inhibition is not coming to a dead stop, otherwise there would be death. Holding up or slowing down prevents catastrophe. It is not only stopping short before you plunge over a cliff, it is also the emotional braking that slows down impulses and actions that repeat the past.

Inhibition is a form of slow motion, altering the rate of metabolism, the speed of an action, the change in direction of an emotion. Paradoxically, inhibition is spontaneity. Stopping encourages the emergence of other actions and other impulses, a chance to reflect on a situation. We can rehearse other possibilities. Internal images would not be possible without this ability to hold back an activity. Inhibition is the core of self-management. This continuum of discrete discrimination in action is the accordion in operation. The HOW exercise quickens and crystalizes our responses. In this way it forms an interior existence.

Of course, too much or too little inhibition can imprison or kill us or bring on over-excitation or boredom. A stance of pride can inhibit defeat or contempt. Aloofness can inhibit contact. With too much inhibition, desires and feelings never surface. Alternately, the lack of inhibition may cause our feelings to overwhelm ourselves or others.

The HOW exercise teaches emotional freedom through inhibition. When presented with the question, what is your image of yourself?, your response should be to inhibit, stop action, and sense the picture of your pose. This is Step One. To experience how you hold yourself is to prevent other possibilities from occurring. Step Two gives the precise events of muscular inhibition that maintain your pose. Inhibition, increasing and decreasing contractions, slowing down the action in Step Three allows Step Four, the emergence of suppressed patterns of feeling. Step Four is the stage of minimal voluntary control of inhibition. At this point the give-and-take of increase and decrease, contraction and expansion are not influenced by conscious decision. In Step Five inhibition becomes your major teacher by supporting new patterns through the practice of voluntary control and by preventing easy return to former patterns.

BRAINSTEM-HINDBRAIN
Inner Organ Layer
The Instinctual Organ
Regulation Brain

SELF-REFLECTION EXERCISE
INHIBITION

1. How do I picture inhibition? (Held-back or not held-back; impulsive or restrained)

2. How do I use myself to be either over or under-inhibited?

3. How do I increase or decrease my inhibition?

4. How do I wait, germinate, let the pause teach me?

5. How do I use my learning to form a new stance of inhibition or return to my old one?

MOTOR MEMORY

In working with the HOW, the ability to invoke simple muscular movements is central. The cerebellum, the major portion of the brain, has the task of retaining and recalling essential muscle movement patterns. Similarly, the brain stem is responsible for smooth organ muscle and the thalamus and cortex for emotional muscular movements.

The self is an ongoing organization of continuous muscle actions called motor patterns. These patterns constitute a fundamental, mostly unconscious leitmotif, a pattern of awareness, much like intuition. We use our muscles yet don't know we are using them. Muscular movement patterns are the source of what we call memory. We think of memory as a recollection of pictures, situations, and emotions, a sort of hologram of the event. In order to produce that hologram experience we recall an actual past muscle pattern together with its emotional associations. By re-experiencing those patterns and associations, we make internal images to represent the event.

This recall action is motor memory. Through motor memory, the event recalled as a pattern of action acts as an organizer for the next level of organization and behavior. This is what links memory and consciousness as well as the past, the present, and the future.

The steps of the HOW process make use of motor memory, intensifying the action of small muscle groups into macroscopic patterns of action. We evoke the already present mini-patterns of motor memory in an intensified form. The resulting muscular action is ancient and modern. The new behavior patterns we establish through the HOW exercise are built upon our experience of the past in the present.

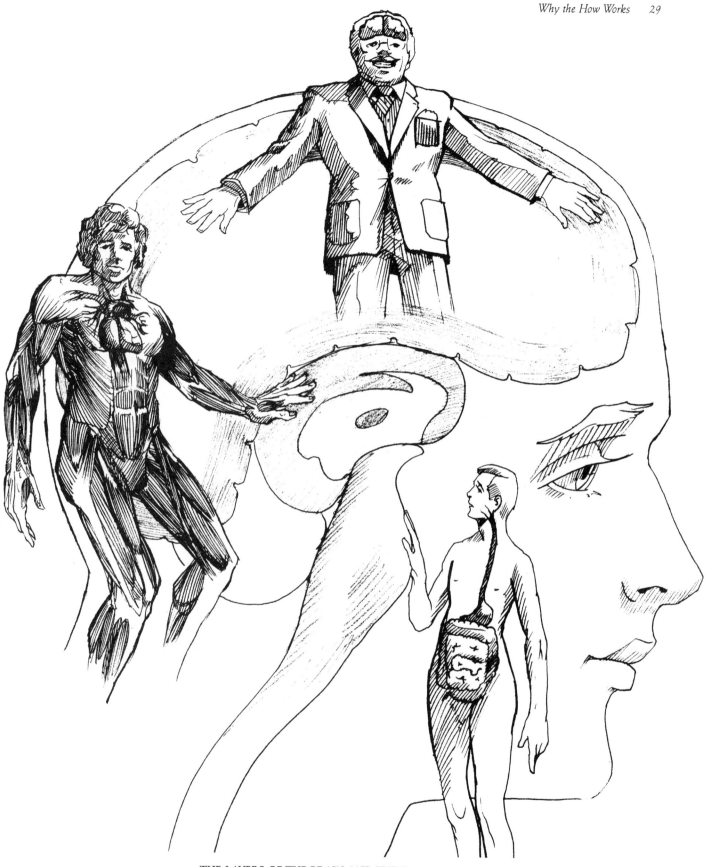

THE LAYERS OF THE BRAIN AND THEIR ASSOCIATED
SYMBOLIC ORGAN SYSTEMS

4 *inner life*

MAN ATTEMPTS to give language to inner experience by using outside objects as analogies for human experience, for example, cave wall paintings, totem poles, or the wearing of animal dress and masks to indicate that he feels like an animal. Stories and poems, myths and dreams are used to express the inner meaning of biology, birth, pregnancy, growth and death. These are attempts to grasp a dimension of existence different from the outward orientation of the senses. The concept of the Five Steps continues this same tradition.

The perception of an inner dimension sheds light on the multilayered dynamics of living environments—families, social situations, individuals. The novelist and playwright focus on this inner dimension when they present the struggles of individual life. This inner dimension is a fundamental theme of modern literature.

The language of inward experience differs from that of the outer world; it uses a different vocabulary. The realm of images, feelings, memories and actions has rules all its own. The HOW process is a way of understanding the connection between inner organization and outer behavior. The challenge is to find a vocabulary that describes what appears to be beyond psychology and biology, but which includes them. The voice of the inner life, expressed as experience, knowledge, and behavior, is the voice of layered organization. The HOW exercise develops a language for experience. It makes a clearing through which process can speak. The physicality of this approach creates connections between the invisible and the visible, between inner feeling and outward behavior. As you live these connections, you find that there is no gap or separation between them; they are aspects of a continuum of experienced existence.

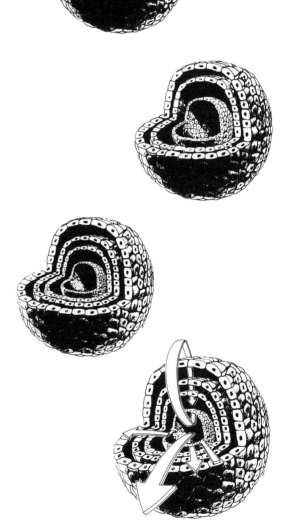

LAYERING OF EXPERIENCE
  The Five Steps as a surface-to-depth phenomenon
  The process of organization and disorganization

CHARACTER

Character manifests consistent organization, an internal logic with its accompanying modes of expression, emotion and action. It is the behavior by which you are known. Its structure is the sum of your personal emotional history as well as universal genetic rules.

Character, like all structure, has layers that function for survival and maintenance, protection and nourishment, growth and reproduction. These layers can be identified in the brain as brain-stem, mid-brain, and cortex, and in the entire body as skin, muscle, viscera, liquids, and bone. Through the HOW exercise you experience layers of structure and their connection to your character.

SELF-REFLECTION EXERCISE
CHARACTER

1. What is the behavior by which I recognize myself or others recognize me? (Friendly, willful, pleasing, serious)

2. What do I do physically to make this behavior?

3. How can I make it more or make it less?

4. What happens to me after I do this?

5. How do I use this learning?

RELATIONSHIPS AND THE FIVE STEPS

While the major focus of this book is on working with one's self, it implies also that others are involved. Ultimately we live and die with others. How we work with ourselves affects others as they, in turn, affect us. In the course of working with our somatic-emotional process, we invoke the interpersonal relationships of the past, present, and those of the future. How we reach out to create closeness or maintain distance, share or withhold our feelings makes our process a human event of warmth or coldness.

Each person forms a dual relationship of contact and connection with themselves and others even as they maintain separation and differentiation. Impulses and desires arise which require self-mastery and then contact with others in order to satisfy them. As a result of the insults we have received, a number of situations may exist—we connect with others but lose our self; we connect solipsistically with ourselves and give up contact with others; we experience uncontrolled urges and become victims to these impulses; or in making contact with others we end up being manipulated by them. The Five Steps are the ritual for maintaining connection, establishing contact, and managing our own feelings and needs.

How we establish connection and contact to be with others can be known through the Five Steps. There is a ritual to establishing connection and contact so that closeness and distance is managed and we remain in control of our own needs and feelings. Each of us starts with a need to connect to others. This contact may be based on instinctual need, social image, or personal choice. Some organize rituals to deny this and substitute duty, obligation, or shoulds for personal contact.

Step One is the image, role, or posture of how we connect to others embodied in a stance of closeness or distance. Step Two and Three is how we extend to another and gather back to ourself, get close and withdraw, stay fused or pull back. Are we obedient and passive, rebellious and defiant? In Step Four we enter the visceral world of non-imagistic roles and actions, connected with ourself and others at a deep level. At this stage we are ready to form another level of relationship either to expand or shorten the contact and connection. This gets enacted in Step Five.

Each of these stages offers challenges that affect our way of relating, generating or resolving conflict. Some of us get stuck trying to relate according to images of safety and propriety. Our own needs get submerged. Alternately we may act out impulsively and not be able to control or direct our impulses so they wash over others and ourselves. We may inhibit, interfere with our impulses until we are a spasm of depression, separate and alone. Or become an unformed, uninhibited, uncontrolling dreamer living in our own fantasy of Stage Four. Maybe we are forever trying to be the right person or change the world; we become a constant stream of connection without ever being pinned down.

> *The secret of transformation is to overcome the old, and make your own way, the goal of maturity.*

SELF-REFLECTION EXERCISE
INTERPERSONAL RELATIONSHIP

1. What is my image of making contact or connecting with others or my response to their attempts to contact me? (Do I want closeness or distance or some combination. Do I generate contact or respond to others' attempts to connect)

2. How do I organize my image, role, or posture around contact and connection?

3. How do I inhibit these images, roles, and postures?

4. How do I exist in an unconditioned connection with myself and wait for a new image of contact to form?

5. How do I regulate my contact with others in a new way, how do I allow myself to be shaped by their demands as well as try to shape their contact with me?

Feelings are the result of cellular pulsations, metabolism, cytoplasmic currents, internal motility. To reach organismic satisfaction feeling must be organized, making links and pathways between liquid organization and muscular behavior. One function of feeling is to communicate deep organismic states, like hunger, love, pain. A second function of feeling is to organize states of awareness and action. In creating continual organization, in seeking expression, feeling becomes form. Form and feeling are thus a continuum from liquidity to solidity, from internal experience to external expression.

In growing up we make form by shaping our feelings. When, as children, we are intimidated or criticized by adults, we slump in, withdraw, shrink, become small. We create a form that communicates smallness or humiliation. Or we respond to criticism with defiance, rebellion, anger or contempt, warding off the attack by stiffening and bracing. Thus, feeling creates our form while form keeps certain feelings intact.

Schools and other institutions understand this connection only too well. Schools teach us to pay attention, our feelings are silenced in order to concentrate on an external authority. This form is created by holding still, stiffening the neck, focusing the eyes, and bracing the head. As we learn this form, we find that inner urges and desires become muted. The military trains soldiers in a stance—chest up, stomach in, spine stiff, and buttocks squeezed—which controls feelings of fear.

This phenomenon of the continuum of feeling and form is at the heart of understanding the nature of emotional life. As adults, we find that we have feelings with few avenues of expression because either our parents or society could not tolerate these feelings, or they never arose. Alternately, our form continues to invoke feelings that no longer have a place, like obedience to authority or feeling small. Or we find ourselves in socially approved roles with little underlying feeling to call our own.

Today many insist that the expression of feelings is primary. However, to what feelings do they refer—feelings based upon present reality or feelings based upon the past? When adults express child-like feelings, adult feelings never develop. Feelings are meant to structure a situation. When feelings represent something unfinished from the past, their present impact is muted. For example, for some, anger is an emotional response meant to restructure a current situation. For others, everyday annoyance automatically generates rage and the perpetuation of childhood memories of impotence. The HOW methodology can disorganize rage and the inner readiness for combat, and permit feelings of annoyance to incubate until other feelings emerge. The ability to contain feelings is as important as the ability to express them.

THE CONTINUITY OF EMOTIONAL EXPRESSION
How Feeling Changes Form

THE CONTINUITY OF EMOTIONAL GESTURE
From Compression to Inflation
From Shrinking to Attack
From Underformed to Overformed

Another problem is feelings without avenues of expression. Some feel the need to cry but cannot. Memory says "be grown up," "you're a big boy (or girl) now," so they stifle the feeling by choking it off. They are stuck in an old organization without a means of completing their feeling either by crying or dismantling the readiness-to-cry form.

Feeling is a continuum of intensity requiring more and more levels of organization. But feeling is also dependent upon form. There is a reciprocal relationship between the differentiation of form and the intensity of feeling. The Five Steps are meant to crystalize this continuum of feeling-form organization and to help when this organization is not appropriate. By establishing reciprocity between form and feeling the HOW exercise maintains the freshness of feeling and the diversity of its expression. The secret connection between form and feeling, one of the deepest mysteries of human existence, is revealed.

EMOTIONAL IDENTITY

Emotion is behavior. Anger, rage, fear, terror, pleasure, joy—all have a clear muscular and visceral shape and require an organized pattern of action. Once the pattern of an organized emotional expression is identified, it is capable of reorganization.

SELF-REFLECTION EXERCISE
EMOTIONAL IDENTITY

1. What is my consistent emotional quality? (Joyful, sad, angry, resigned, bitter)

2. How do I organize this emotion?

3. How do I intensify or release it?

4. How do I permit the upwelling of other emotion?

5. How do I shape new emotional qualities or return to what is familiar?

THE DEFENSE AGAINST EMOTIONAL TRUTH

Everyone wants to avoid pain and insult, rejection and belittlement. In doing the HOW exercise you discover how you defend yourself somatically against past insults. Defenses based upon past emotional rejections and disappointments prevent direct emotional responses and shapings in the present. Defensive reactions become self images, for example, "I am invulnerable," and become part of how performance is organized. "I will do this perfectly, I will use myself with a straight spine and impeccable coordination." Sometimes fear prevents new attempts to organize. Waiting is also a defense. Procrastination prevents moving towards the world again.

SELF-REFLECTION EXERCISE
EMOTIONAL DEFENSE

1. How do I defend myself against the repetition of past insults? (Stiffen, smile, threaten, give in)

2. What do I do to create this posture?

3. How can I undo it by making it more or making it less?

4. What happens when I wait?

5. Can I be present without my old defenses, or do I return to them?

MULTILAYERED REALITY

Our shape is a multilayered reality, each layer a structure of inner and outer reality. One of these layers is impersonal, genetic, non-volitional. One layer is societal, traditional, imitative. One layer is personal, subjective, volitional. I call the three layers: prepersonal, postpersonal, and personal.

The prepersonal is inherited, genetic experience—anatomy, gender—and appetites. This is the given of existence. The postpersonal represents tradition—the experiences of family, school, work, society, culture. We are trained in the rules of all these realms and then practice, imitate, perpetuate, and perfect them. Finally, the personal layer represents the way we embody, take possession of the prepersonal and post-personal experiences, give ourselves personal identity, use ourselves to make a private and personal shape.

These layers form what we call our self. We have an instinctual form, a shape that nature makes to express genderedness and insure adult survival. How we form our instincts, or how they form us is seen in the shape and behavior we live out. How society forms us as polite, competitive, rational is also seen in the forms, roles, and postures we act in public, toward strangers, with friends, at work, when we are with others. Then there is the constructed self, an organization of events crystalizing the experiences of these two worlds. Our personal layer begins as a unique, individuated response to the other layers.

There is a powerful relationship between the three layers
—the prepersonal, the postpersonal, and the personal. How
these layers connect and communicate with each other is
the business of the formative process and, in particular, the
Five Steps.

The connection and contact between the layers offers us
a blueprint of ourselves, a sense of "I," or "me." If our
process is objectified, put outside, distanced, it becomes
"not I." Distancing the experiences of any layer of ourselves
makes us believe we are different from our formative self.
We begin to believe the objectified and stereotyped internal
image as our real self. We then "have a self," rather than "be
a self-making process."

Any layer may exercise too much or too little control. If
the societal layer has too much control, we become over-
civilized, robot-like. If the societal layer has too little control,
we become impulse ridden. If a personal self is lacking we
over-identify with either our social conditioning or our
instinctual images and urges. Alternately, we may so over-
control ourselves that we lose contact with the prepersonal
and end up self-centered. For some, the outer layer crushes
the inner layer by becoming overinflamed. For others, the
outer layer is unformed and instinct or the private self runs
wild.

Steps Two and Three of the Five Steps, organization and
disorganization, make connections and contact between the
layers of ourselves and the forms that either make this possible
or inhibit it. Steps Two and Three, organization and disorganization, expansion-contraction, intensifying-deintensifying,
open the door for volition and reflex action indicating how
contact and connection are made or formed.

Steps Two and Three generate sensations and feelings,
increase and decrease the river of proprioceptor messages
brought about by the change in organ and muscle shape and
thereby construct a new body image. We focus on the boundaries of our somatic world, we contact, intensify, structure
and destructure and thereby deepen our layered experience.
This process of brain-mind muscle-mind cooperation is a
dialogue by which the organism teaches itself about making
the impersonal or collective personal.

In working with this method we discover the layers of
our process—from posture, to attitude, to expression, to
forming an expression. We go from the pulsations of the
involuntary, to the personal organization of feelings and
emotions, to the forms of action and meaning. We disorganize the given and reorganize a more complex intimate
expression. We move from performance, to inhibiting performance, to taking apart the performance, to the reorganization of performance.

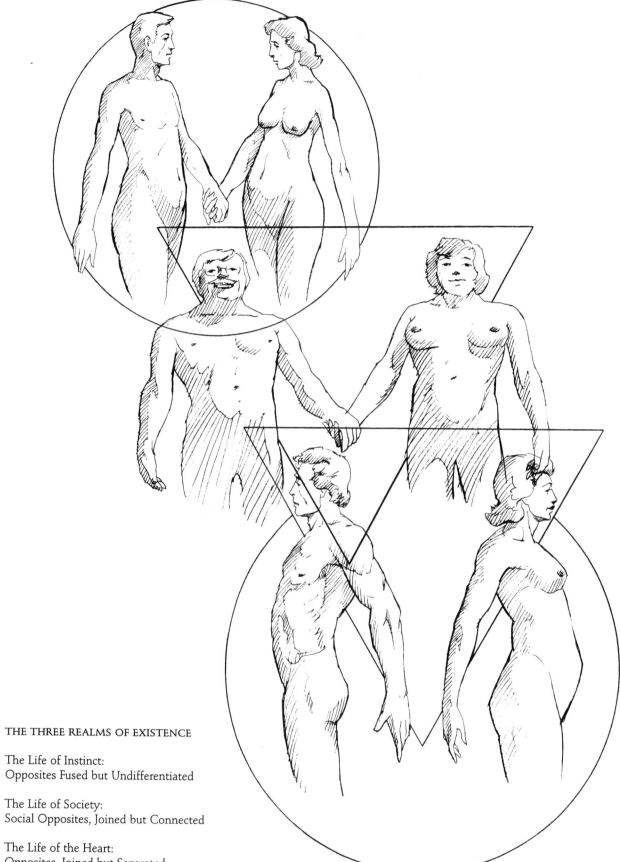

THE THREE REALMS OF EXISTENCE

The Life of Instinct:
Opposites Fused but Undifferentiated

The Life of Society:
Social Opposites, Joined but Connected

The Life of the Heart:
Opposites, Joined but Separated

On the prepersonal level
we experience the Five Steps
as not a part of us,
something that just happens,
the given of nature,
what is.

On the postpersonal level
we experience process
as belonging to others,
society, institutions,
the state, our family.
Our process is shared
theirs and ours,
it is the socialization
of biology.

On the personal level
process is experienced
as our own;
on the other levels
process possesses us
but here we possess process.
The experience is ours.
It is the personalization
of biology.

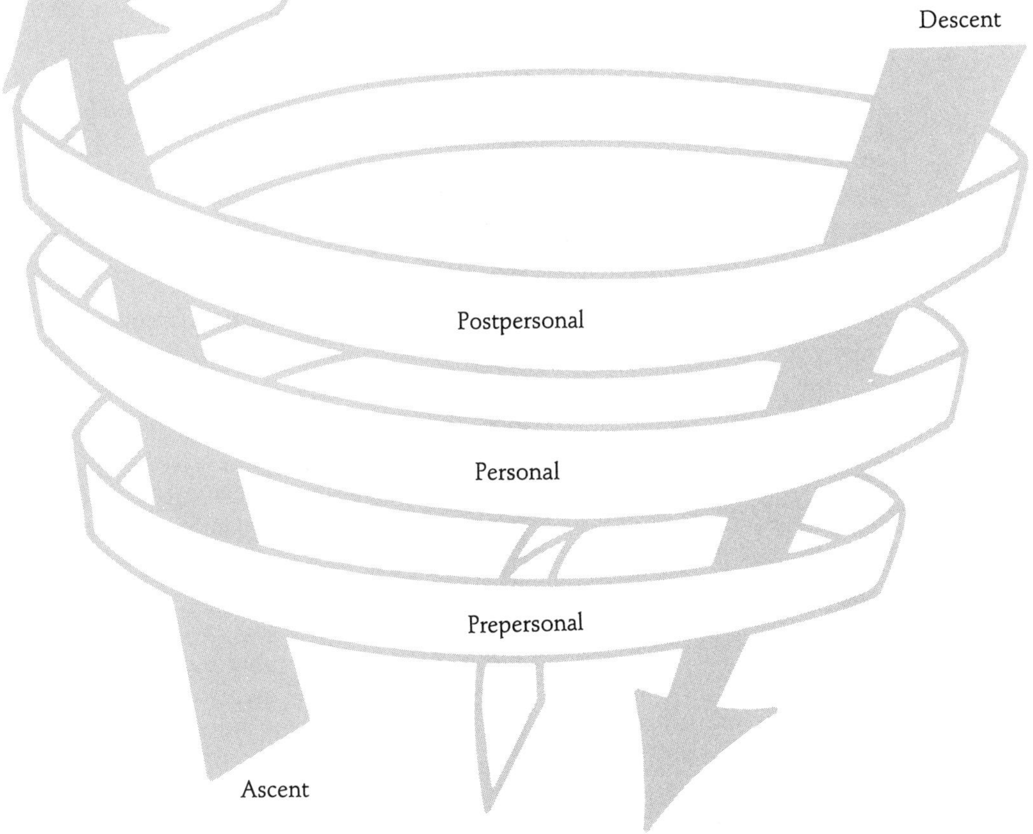

Descent

Postpersonal

Personal

Prepersonal

Ascent

THE CONNECTION OF THE THREE REALMS:
THE ORGANIZATION OF THE SELF

1. Which of my layers do I experience as overactive or underactive? (Instinctual, social, personal)

2. What is the physical organization of this over-activity or under-activity?

3. How do I intensify these organizations?

4. How do I pause, become receptive, let another layer form a voice?

5. How do I apply what I have learned?

THE ROLE OF THE PULSATING CURRENT

The ocean of sensations coming from the rhythms of pulsation are our matrix, a geometry that the brain cells make into shapes representing the prepersonal, societal, and personal levels.

Pulsation is the basic self. It is a current with waves that generate desire, feelings, ideas, actions. Pulsation is a prepersonal inheritance. It builds an outer layer into a membrane and container separating outside from inside. In this way the current becomes layered, and the outer can speak to the inner. So begins feedback, dialogue, self-talk. The human dimension emerges. The outside in dialogue with the inside creates a response that stablizes our associations and memories, concepts and actions, and gives us a personal sense. This forming of a private self is monumental. Forming another layer regulates a dualistic existence and personalizes an impersonal life. We now have a triad instead of a dyad.

From protoplasmic pulsations, or basic animate organization we form a kinetic morphology. This moving, forming shape expanding its experience of its layers finally creates a personalizing of it. Our responses are no longer mere appetites or social commandments but a personal experience of forming a life.

The pulsatory continuum is a basic experience of life, organizing and disorganizing structures that represent it. This is revealed by the Five Steps. Intensification and de-intensification brings forth memories of events, action, situations and then recreates a space to expand yesterday into tomorrow. The pulsatory process becoming a wave, a repeating circulating peristaltic wave, organizes form and assimilates the contents of its environment to distill and transfer these contents to itself. This self generation is the protoplasmic self, kinetic morphology, emotional shape. It is desire on the move, organizing the hungers and experiences of existence into shapes that endure and communicate. Our sense of "I" becomes a moving process, forming and reforming the shape of self.

Pressure is involved in all of performing. When asked to do a task, we put pressure on ourselves. "Stop crying," "be good," are examples of this. To do these things we have to pressure ourselves, withhold impulses, inhibit our way of doing something. We may feel threatened by our hungers, our responses, anger, sadness, sexual feelings. We try to squeeze ourselves into an image for others to approve. We create pressure on the different layers—socially, personally, instinctually. We inhibit one form to facilitate another.

Here is a simple exercise to experience layered reality and Steps Two, Three, and Four. Pressure or squeeze your head. How do you do this? Pressure it more. Now soften it a bit. How do you do this? Squeeze it tighter by involving your eyes. Now let them soften. Pressure your head more by involving your mouth, brain, neck. Make them tighter, then tighter, then softer, then more tight, them more soft, then as tight as you can—a knot of contraction. Now soften it a bit, let go of what you created, soften it more, pause, wait, then relax all of the tension. Repeat all of these steps in sequence several times.

In this simple exercise you organize form as pressure and then disorganize form by giving up pressure. As you do this, you may be able to recognize the social form, the outer layer, the first tightening as restraint, social mask, obedience, concentration, performance; the second level, or middle layer as caution, danger, controlling anger; and the third or prepersonal layer as deep shock, hibernation, the reflex of terror. As you disorganize you give up shock, caution, and restraint. As you go through the pressure exercise whether with the head, or the chest, or the pelvis, you recognize pressure, more pressure, less pressure; form, more form, less form; social, personal, and instinctual layers. You form an experience of the pulsatory continuum and discover that organization and form are related as you move from social control, to personal control, to reflex control.

SOMATIC IMAGE

A somatic image is an anatomical or behavioral form. Skeletal muscles are responsible for posture, learned social roles and instinctual gestures. They make a motif of sensations that give a body image, an external somatic image. The pattern of visceral motility gives rise to sensations that establish an internal somatic image.

Every somatic image has both an internal aspect and an external aspect. There is a part that faces outward towards the world and a part that is knowable only from the inside. For example, the gestures of anger—a fist, loud voices—are external images that signal fight or flight. Internally, adrenaline increases and blood pressure rises. Male and female sexual

PRESSURE
Increase and decrease

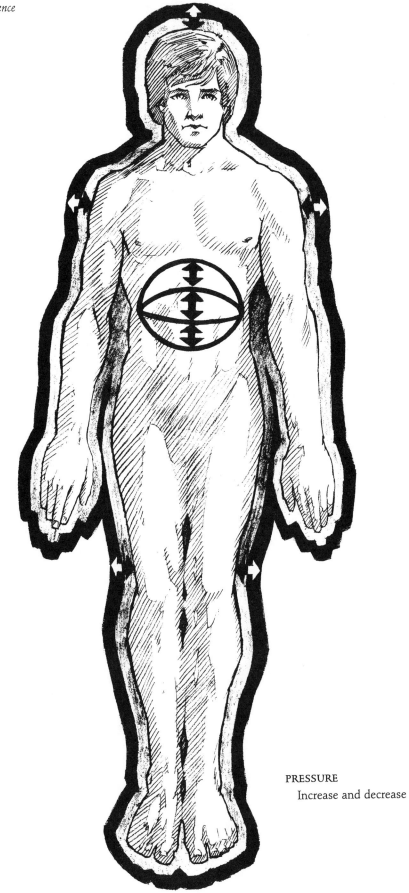

PRESSURE
Increase and decrease

forms are somatic images with external and internal mani-
festations. Outwardly the organization of body posture,
muscles, and expressions produce images that others understand and respond to. The somatic image of another indicates
their intentions as well as their internal state.

Internally we communicate through images. There are
certain recognizable biochemical patterns, such as the hormonal configurations of sexual arousal, anger, or fear, that
inform the brain and the rest of the organism about the
need for appropriate organization. Rushes of adrenaline
change internal chemical and molecular geometry from
being at rest to being fearfully aroused.

Internal and external images communicate with each
other, although we often separate them through denial and
conflict. The interior is fearful, yet the outside looks calm
and reserved. Our heart may be racing yet we hold still and
our face remains calm. The internal message of "be still" or
"get ready to flee" has an external expression of holding.

A somatic image, then, contains inner organ sensations
and emotional configurations as well as body stances and
action poses. A somatic image not only tells the world who
you are, it also tells you who you are.

SELF-REFLECTION EXERCISE
VISIBLE SOMATIC IMAGE

1. What is my persistant visible somatic image? (Confident,
   reserved, relaxed, withdrawn, arrogant, submissive)

2. What do I do muscularly to make this somatic pose?

3. How can I make it more or less intense?

4. What happens when I destructure my habitual somatic
   pose?

5. How do I use myself to form a different somatic image or
   do I return to my former one?

SELF-REFLECTION EXERCISE
INTERIOR SOMATIC IMAGE

1. What consistent somatic image do I recognize from the
   inside? (Agitated, still, hard, rushed, exposed, soft, heavy)

2. What do I do to make this somatic-feeling image?

3. How can I make it more or less intense?

4. What happens in the pause when I inhibit my habitual
   internal somatic form?

5. How do I return to my original internal somatic image or
   use myself to form a new one?

Most of us are not aware of inward experience; neither do we believe that the "kingdom of heaven" is within. We live our lives through public images and external actions. We identify with social performance, not an internal truth. Modern industrial existence encourages the development of the exterior. It is a luxury for many people to form an inner life. While the ability to function externally enhances self-esteem, self-identity, and security, the need for a well-developed inner space is not equally recognized. To solve the problems of everyday life it is necessary to create and defend a private space.

The Five Steps create an inner life. In Step Three, when we deconstitute form, we create a pause, a breath, a synaptic junction waiting for impulses to build. When they do, we are in Step Four, primary process. Descent from the cortex brings either the emotions of the mid-brain or the basic processes of the brain stem. At this pause feelings and internal sensation dominate, pictures and symbols diminish, and insight and images come together as motor action patterns. This hiatus organizes novel responses to situations.

We know through direct action—we do something—and the self-reflecting mind perceives what was done and practices it over and over. Or we present a dreamlike image of an already-completed form of behavior to the inner self-reflecting center. The entire muscular system then imitates the image, organizing a behavior which we then practice. We either reconceive a problem, reorganize what we are going to do with it, or find a way to reorganize ourselves.

The important question is how we create a space and wait for the organization of a response. This response turns out to be who we are. We build an interior, an inside, a bodily form not given by birth. This inner dimension is what religious movements mean by creating a soul or finding a spiritual self. There is a moment in our inner space when polarization and conflict exist in which we create a new organization, one that has not existed before.

SELF-REFLECTION EXERCISE
CREATING AN INNER SPACE

1. How do I create an inner space? (Stop external action, talk to myself, silence my habitual feelings)

2. How do I do this muscularly?

3. How do I intensify this or make it less?

4. How do I pause, wait, let something be created?

5. Do I return to my habitual activity or practice creating a form from what I have learned?

The HOW exercise connects the inside and outside and explores the various levels and layers of existence. Often thinking and feeling seem unrelated. We do things yet don't know why we do them. What we do seems unconnected to inner body sensations, images, or self-perception.

Somatic process is a continuum of images from molecular configurations through hormonal and neural patterns to muscular gestures that become social acts. This multileveled process moves from inside to outside or from our surface to our depths. There is a continuum of connection from the biochemical level to the muscular level, from the subjective to the concrete. Images vary between outer body and inner body, slow or fast paced, archetypal and personal, those given us by nature, those socially learned, and, finally self-selected images. We often split the mind from the body rather than accept this continuum of living process, the many layers of existence.

The Five Steps start at the outside, the outer surface of localization, differentiation, and control, where society and rationality rule. It moves to the middle layers or organs and muscles where self-management and volition dominate and then on to the mysterious depths of Step Four where God rules. At this place there is a mixture of globality, unpredictability, spontaneity as well as order and form. From this inner layer we return to the surface.

SELF-REFLECTION EXERCISE
THE DEPTH TO SURFACE CONTINUUM

1. At what layer do I enter the continuum? (External roles or internal images)

2. How do I create this internal or external organization or perpetuate it?

3. How do I increase or decrease this organization, destructure my starting point and experience its deeper aspects?

4. In the pause, how do other aspects of my organization—dreams, associations, insights, feelings—speak?

5. How do I use this learning? Do I return to my habitual starting point or incorporate, through practice, more of myself?

DESCENT AND ASCENT

A corollary of the inner-outer continuum is the metaphor of ascent and descent, the mythological journey to the underworld and back. In individuals it is the movement between wakefulness and sleep or lying down to standing.

As my earlier books *The Human Ground* and *Your Body Speaks Its Mind* elaborate, the upright stance is a resistance to the pull of gravity. Yet each individual stance also reflects the emotional history of how we were treated as children, with fear or shame, joy or terror.

In the Five Steps of the HOW exercise we descend and ascend; we travel downward, lower our center of gravity, return to the abdominal-pelvic world, and then attempt to rise again. Step One begins with an upright image. Step Two reveals how we keep this image intact. Step Three begins the descent into the underworld, a release from the demands of social performance. We come to a place where structure is more liquid. We allow the geysers of emotion and vision to project themselves toward the light. Step Four involves symbolical, psychological, emotional, and somatic experiences. This starts our ascent, the unconscious becomes more conscious, forming itself in the world, which we reach in Step Five. We leave cortical brain existence to return to our roots in the autonomic nervous system and brain stem. When nourished, we return to the world of wakefulness. This ascension or return to uprightness is accompanied by new images, memories, and feelings.

SELF-REFLECTION EXERCISE
ASCENT AND DESCENT

1. Where am I fixated on ascent or descent? (Braced against the world or collapsing under it)

2. How do I use my muscles to create my stance? What do I actually do to form this organization?

3. How can I make it more and make it less? What are the sensations of disorganization and descent, or more organization and ascent?

4. In the pause, how do I experience my descent? How do I live with what is emerging?

5. How do I use what I have learned? Do I continue in a habitual ascent or descent or do I attempt to form something from what I have learned?

In descending we return to our common ground, a universal layer. Thought is feeling, intense tranquil configurations of pure energy, an ocean with its secrets as our core, a deep intuition. Step Four is a spaceless existence in the abdominal-pelvic world as opposed to the world of performance of Step One. It is the arena of the unrehearsed. From here come solar flares, oceanic upwellings, projections of feeling to mobilize internal vision which brain and muscles then organize.

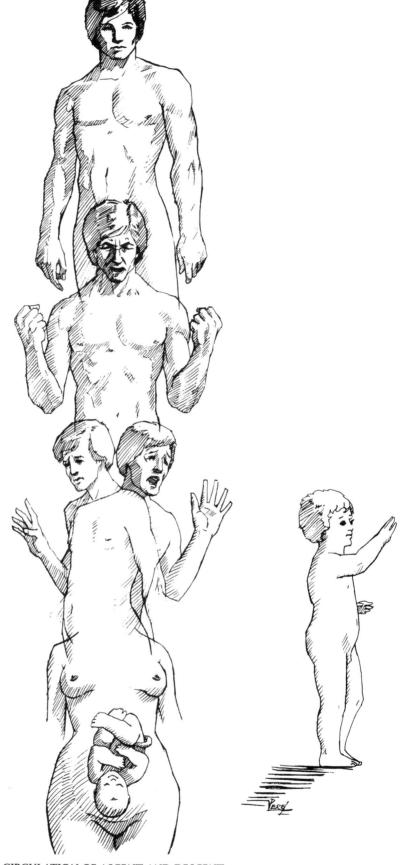

THE CIRCULATION OF ASCENT AND DESCENT

stories and somagrams

ALL OF US create stories and myths to make sense of existence, individually and collectively. Stories help us come to terms with the mystery of our existence as a body, and fill the space of the internal and external unknown. Our genetic organization makes a story, telling us how to form bodies. Society tells us, through stories, how to behave. And stories are written by each of us as we survive, grow, and individuate. We tell ourselves a story as a way to rationalize or make sense out of some event, or to give ourselves a way to act.

The creation of stories is an integrative function bringing together known elements of experience and connecting them with inventive or imaginative elements. Order, sense, meaning, continuity of organization and form is maintained through a story. We have an ability to create inner and outer reality, in dreams, epic poems, dramas, novels, motion pictures, paintings, dance, or personal stories.

We organize stories about our past, present, and future. These stories are belief systems which perpetuate bodily and psychological shape. Stories not only describe present life situations, they help us rehearse future actions. They enable us to inhibit or give up present actions when they become dangerous. Stories tell muscles to get ready and then to do something. They tell us how to wait, dream, and reorganize by inhibiting our present internal signals, allowing a new drama to emerge.

Stories are organizers of action, gathering together the experiences we have, generating a continuity about what has happened so the rest of the organism can organize an appropriate shape to generate contact, survival, and community.

A story is an experience of organized bodily responses. It involves muscular patterns of too much or too little form, too much or too little excitation. Living events organize a stream of sensations and actions, first in the language of biochemical elements, then in the language of emotions, then as the structure of one's developmental history, and then as a personal story. All of these events are the same event, occuring on many levels.

A story carries an external message ("I am a martyr," "I dominate others," "I am miserable") that reflect an inner dialogue of images, words, symbols, and sensations that arise from internalized previous history. Memory is made up of these muscular and excitatory patterns. These patterns are history enacted in the present. They may be coordinated or uncoordinated. To disorganize the memory of a particular story the muscular and excitatory pattern as well as the emotional associations must be taken apart.

If our story makes basic order, we can then ask, "How do we form our story?" "How does our story, through its feedback mechanism, form us?" "How can we inhibit the story we perpetually tell ourselves and allow a different story to emerge?" "How does our story organize order and meaning in our lives?" Our story can be found in dreams, images, thoughts, fantasies, as well as actions. At the end of our life, we are the story we have embodied. We form a life even if we forfeit many opportunities. We have formed bonds of closeness or distance with others, satisfied or not satisfied our desires, become heroes or clowns, winners or losers.

STORY-TELLING

Internal dialogue forms our body image. This image comes from the cellular feelings and the sensations of bones, muscles, and organs. Like a radar screen makes an image of a moving object, internal organization forms an image or story. We organize inner and outer space according to our emotional relationship to others as well as ourself. We know how big or small we are and whether to move towards or away from others. Over-indulgent parents make us feel bigger than we are, rejecting ones make our life space smaller. Angry, eruptive parents make us pull back and brace or blow up to inflate our space. When humiliated, we protect ourselves through becoming small and compact. Body image is emotional experience concretized as our shape both internally and in the space we take up externally.

We talk to ourselves, carrying on a conversation with pictures of our sensations, feelings, and in words. We compare, measure, place, judge and rationalize. Whether we know it or not, we tell ourselves a story, a story that connects to feelings and our struggle to form ourselves.

At first, our story is given to us. "You are inadequate, unworthy, stupid, not deserving of love." These messages originate in the dawn of consciousness. It makes no difference that someone outside of us said, "You are a bad child," because we end up telling it to ourselves and perpetuating it as a body image.

By using the Five Steps you may discover the internal organization of your story. The first step concerns the nature of your story and how you tell it. How you tell your story to yourself and to others involves an image. "What a terrible childhood I had," you say, and collapse in defeat or become rigid in rebellion. The goal is to feel your internal organization, the steps of how you use yourself, and how this organization gives rise to meaning, associations, memories, emotions and actions.

When you engage in the HOW exercise, you recall past organization. This remembering allows for disorganization and reorganization. "Stiffen, be proud, don't cry." The story you tell yourself deepens as you learn how previous experience as present structure is organized. It is a powerful way to communicate, share, and integrate knowledge and experience as well as a means of creating personal reality.

> *Process moves*
> *from what has happened,*
> *to what is,*
> *to what can be,*
> *until it becomes*
> *what will be.*

CASE STUDIES

In these cases two clients describe in their own words their story and how it gives them an image with which they meet the world, how they become dissatisfied with it and begin to create a new one through using themselves differently. They invoke the Five Steps to form a new response, rather than returning to their habitual ones.

JIM
THE "DOER"

I am a doer. I've discovered that I have a self-imposed requirement to perform, that is, to meet someone else's expectations and ignore my own needs. This includes always having the correct answer to any questions I might be asked, a learned attitude that has been with me as long as I can remember. This mode of using myself has effectively cut me off from my own feelings and from my bodily self.

I created a body image—stiff-spined, tight-bellied, polite—and, in time, this body form of the "doer" took charge of my life. I was always, I thought, doing for others, never experiencing the appreciation I expected, and hence feeling driven to redouble my doing.

JIM
THE DOER

Perception of this process first became evident to me in a dream. In this dream I threw away my rigid body form and started walking from the hips instead of from the shoulders in a powerful, masculine way. Even in the dream I could feel the difference in my muscles and skeleton. Later I began to apply the HOW methodology. By asking myself how I accomplished this new way of walking, I learned to identify the process whereby I put my body into a rigid, uptight form with the consequent rigid behavior.

First, I identified the feeling quality of the rigid, uptight body image (*step one*). With this image I felt how rigidly I was holding myself or how stiffly I was walking, or noticed that I had a stiff neck. Second, I slowly learned how I did this to myself. In response to a question or a request to do something, I would almost instantly prepare myself not to fail by stiffening my spine, squeezing my buttocks and genitals, pulling my chest up and away from my belly, and puffing out my chest, going into shallower breathing and tightening my diaphragm (*step two*). Third, I used the "accordion exercise" in two primary ways to learn about undoing myself (*step three*). One was to inhale deeply and to willfully tighten my diaphragm muscles—making it super-tight as only a good "doer" can—and then let out my breath in four distinct exhales, while simultaneously relaxing the diaphragm muscles in four steps. In this way, I learned, over a period of time, to experience what being non-rigid in the diaphragm felt like, and eventually I could produce a comfortable, non-rigid form at will when I recognized that I was being uptight.

Another "accordion" exercise I used when I wanted to deflate my heroic, compulsive stance was to fill my lungs, raise my shoulders to my ears, hold this position briefly, and then slowly exhale and let my shoulders down at the same time, feeling myself all the way into my pelvis. The effect was again to undo my uptight, rigid form and to allow me to find a more alive form.

Both these interventions have gradually reformed or reorganized my body and how I use myself (*step four*). This happened by reorganizing my rigidity, intervening with it, and learning to identify the quality of the feeling of the non-rigid me, so that I slowly learned how I can produce it.

The final step for me is the emergence of a new form (*step five*). In my case, my shoulders and chest have softened visibly, my back is less rigid and my belly is fuller. With this new form, there comes a new story for myself. I no longer feel compelled to be the "doer." I allow myself to be reflective, to write, and not get uptight if I cannot do something or if my old model suddenly reasserts itself. I am learning to make a new shape for myself, to structure my life differently.

As a computer operator I often experience my process while working at the machine and gain a deeper sense of how I am organized in patterns of receiving and extending myself.

For the past few years I have worked in an office doing data and word processing. Producing quality work requires that I develop certain technical skills. In the process of working towards these skills, the way I sit at the computer is an important feedback mechanism for how I am using myself (*step one*). Often my posture seems forced and pushed. When I stop and ask myself how am I doing that, I can feel how I am squeezing in my belly and pulling up my shoulders, rounding my chest over my belly, trying to create strength. I tell myself to slow down and sink back into the chair to relax. After a while, when I prepare to type again, I make up a game—how relaxed can I be and still hit the keys. I let my legs and seat feel heavy in the chair, I feel gravity as my arms and shoulders extend to type (*step two*). My breath feels soft in my belly. Now, how am I going to move and create enough pressure to set the keys in motion? I feel the parallels with the social world—some boundaries have to be formed to let movement begin; contact involves pressure; interaction means moving. As I work, the dialogue begins to develop. How am I moving? Tensely! What is my relationship to that? Dissatisfied! How do I end it (*step three*)? Stop, let it go, pause a moment. Then I see how far I can move, practicing the new, less tense way. Again and again, I feel the habitual tension pattern beginning to form and creep up my torso. Stop and bring it down (*step two versus step three*). Oh, now I realize that as soon as I lift my arms, before I type a sentence, I have firmed my belly, stiffened my neck, arm, shoulders. Try again, keep breathing. This time my arm feels heavier as my fingers touch the keys. But when I begin to type faster I notice that my rib cage is tensing up, as is my upper arm. How do I bring my arms back to myself instead of tensing? The motion they have is basically to extend away from my torso as I begin to type and then tighten up as I go fast. In experimenting I've learned that I extend my arms fully, but I hold my elbows out in a way that creates pressure on the keyboard. I don't come back to myself but remain semi-extended and locked in a tense position.

In the next few days, I felt this same movement pattern in other activities (*step five*). I also realized that this pattern has a history and links me to my past. With my boyfriend, I felt a reaching out with my head and neck. After that, I realized that I never really relaxed my neck. Similarly with

SARAH
OVER-EXTENSION

my co-workers, I found out that once I brought myself out with enthusiasm and responses to them, I had to make a few pauses to take a deep breath or quit holding onto my torso so firmly. I had difficulty in maintaining self-contact in the midst of interaction. In all three experiences, I felt how being semi-extended narrowed my boundaries and created a cramped feeling. I recognize this as having gone on my whole life—seeking contact yet failing. This is my story.

As these two case studies show, for a person to work with himself and his story, he must start with Step One, the image he has of himself, the situation he is in, the story he tells himself and others. As he works through to Step Five, he understands the structure of his story and disorganizes it. With Step Five comes the possibility of creating a new story.

SOMAGRAMS

Another way to know your process is to make a picture, an image, a somagram. Somagrams are somatic-emotional images that reveal a public or a private layer. With this image you can capture, realistically or symbolically, the feeling of your story. You project the qualities of your inner experience, making visible your somatic-emotional state. As images accumulate over time, more of your past and present is available.

Somagrams, then, are images that portray your story. They are projective statements about the nature of your organization. They show a present situation, how you feel inside, where you hurt, need help, what you think and feel about yourself. With a series of somagrams you could map your past.

Sensations and organ movements are organized in patterns. Pulsations give continuity, shape, and somatic order. Somatic shape is the basis of thoughts, feelings, action. The brain organizes and forms pictures, symbols, and shapes to organize form and meaning. Somagrams, therefore, are a natural language.

Somagrams are projections of process. In making emotional visualizations, we incorporate and reorganize experience. Somagrams encourage and teach another way to form the self. They point to our pain and our problems, depicting how we are vital and animated, constricted and compressed, deadened and confused. Somagrams reveal areas of conflict in a person's present form, overbound or underbound, over-excited or under-stimulated.

To draw a somagram depict yourself as you experience yourself, not as an accurate work of art. Somagrams are not idealizations, fantasies, or mirror reflections but attempts to let your imagination reflect emotional organization. Use the HOW exercise to work with what you discover. How do I restrict my neck or head? How do I keep myself a "good boy" by cutting off my neck and keeping my internal fire localized? Somagrams are not concerned with how you appear to others, but how you organize.

Somagrams are the way we know ourselves, the message we send to the world, and the demand we make to others about how to receive us. As a pictoral image, the somagram captures present organization. As a series of images, taken over a day or a longer period of time, somagrams capture the themes of a life.

CASE STUDIES

The following somagrams were made by people who have been clients. Each writes a story to accompany his somagram and uses the Five Steps to intensify his somagram, to identify his patterns of organization, and to create the experiences of disorganization and reorganization.

JOEL

I am in my thirties, I have never married. Previous to my current relationship, I pursued women who eventually rejected me. Presently, I am involved with a woman who seeks as much contact from me as I am willing to provide. Throughout our nine-month relationship I have had an inner desire to rebel against this monogamous type of involvement. This desire is expressed (Somagram 1) by dark strokes. Internally, I feel a fire, a wildness. The dark black lines around my shoulders, throat, and sides contain the wild person. I give myself messages, "behave yourself," "be good," "don't act that way," "don't do anything wild." I was brought up in a family where wild behavior was unbefitting to someone of our social position.

My second somagram (Somagram 2) shows a situation where a woman wants to befriend me and appreciates the fact that I am warm and caring but shows no sexual desire for me. While this situation is a normal one, I experience it as rejection, a further wounding of a fragile ego. This somagram shows my ingrained pattern of insult that is susceptible to feeling violated. I still expect to get something that I never received in my early years. As a teen I imagined all my peers proving their manhood by sexual exploits, while I had none. I watched from the sidelines, engraving upon myself an image of sexual inferiority. Presently, I keep this feeling, but add to it an inner statement of anger, "Who needs you, I don't care if you think I am a nice person, I am not a fox just waiting to get out of his cage."

Thou shalt not
Lead a good, well-behaved life
Be like Dad, don't look at other women
Keep it in

Let me out
I want to be like everyone else,
to play, live, be joyful

I will
Freedom
Not to be trapped by a woman

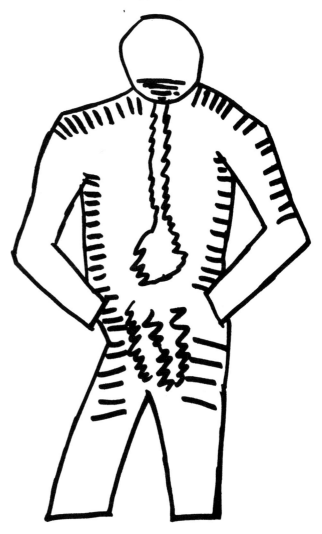

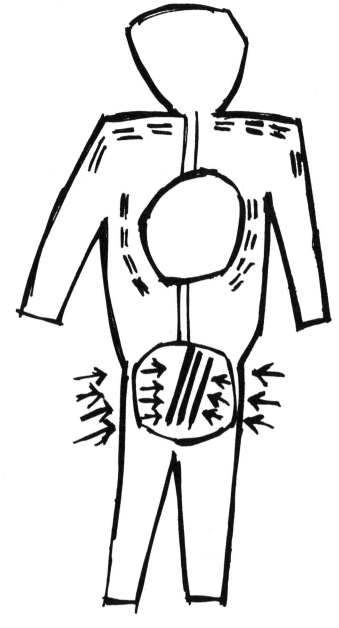

Nice, warm,
Kind-hearted,
A good person

Emotional virus and bacteria

Ingrained patterns of insult,
discredited and invalidated

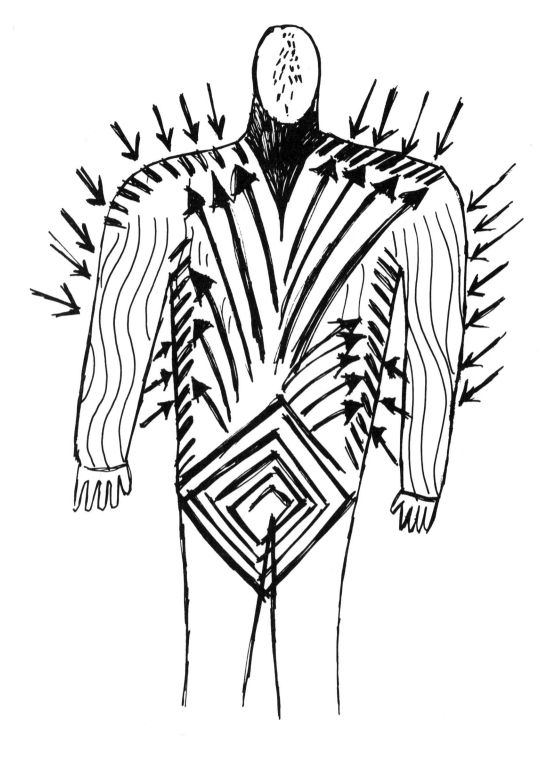

Wild impulses
Limits of integrity

I drew a third somagram during a recent seminar where I experienced strong impulses inside my torso that seemed to want to reach to the skin surface and beyond (the inner black arrows). At times these impulses felt overwhelming. In response, I blocked and hardened myself. These are the black lines in my neck, throat, and sides. These lines keep my wildness inside tolerable limits and prevent invading forces from taking over my inner integrity.

My current relationship manifests these conflicts. At times, our contact is warm and intimate. I can sustain that warmth for periods not exceeding twenty-four hours. Then I have a strong feeling that too much of her is getting into me. I become scared that I will have to make a commitment to her. I thicken myself and totally withdraw. I go back to the seclusion of my apartment to re-establish equilibrium. There I begin to tell myself, "you should not withdraw," "you should be able to maintain contact," "what is wrong with you?" This is self-defeating since the more I force myself into contact because I am "supposed to," the more revulsion I feel. I am trapped in a permanent situation, not permitting any woman to get too close. This is shown in the lines that encase my pelvis. The statement of this area is, "I will stay this way," "you cannot penetrate either from outside or from the inner radiance in my chest." I feel a bull-like stubborn refusal to yield and then an unconscious confusion of not knowing how to yield.

When I was able to use the HOW to destructure my rigidity, I felt great pleasure. With the Five Steps I learned concretely how I withdraw, in gradations. I am offered an alternative other than total contact or total withdrawal. When I am in a situation that becomes uncomfortable for me, I am able to experience my withdrawal and take some control over my own process. I become aware of how I withdraw from eye contact. I experience the moving of my neck and the turning of my head. This reduces the intensity of contact. I then can reverse this movement and make eye contact again, and not turn off my emotions. I can choose the level of contact that I can sustain and not be a victim to either numb isolation or overwhelming excitation.

Working with my somagrams and the HOW steps means to disorganize the tensions in my pelvis and neck, to let myself down, and inhibit the inflammation of the pelvis. As I organize my wildness into loving behavior, I integrate strength and tenderness, and become a wild man who has been civilized rather than one who has been tamed.

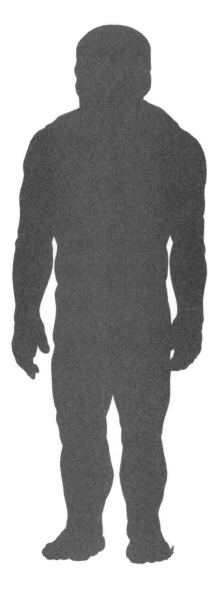

JOEL

Recently, I became aware of how my back felt like a board, stiffened and flat with a couple of hinges separating the planes. I drew the following somagram and this is how I interpret it. I would say that my "story" is that I feel great need for contact. This longing I experience primarily in my chest and stomach. My upper half is organized to inhibit my reaching out. My bottom half is solid, so I can do anything from there. My back is ready for action but I can't "move." It stiffens in a painful, "I want," reaching out but pulling back. I think I use my shoulder incorrectly, I reach out like an automaton, with an "ideal" of what to do, rather than acting directly from my heart. My use of myself is stiff and incomplete.

When I was with my boyfriend I would deeply relax and these patterns of pain would let go. I also use the HOW exercise to relax, I hunch over from the front of the chest and intensify it and begin to destructure the "bending over." I begin to experience the elements of disorganization if I do this slowly enough. As I do this frequently I have a memory of bracing when my mother verbally assaulted me. It was a two-sided response—on the one hand I would shrink and distance myself—yet on the other hand I would fight, push her away internally, ward her off. In a certain way I didn't want her near me, I didn't want to be vulnerable.

As I do the Five Steps I realize that both aspects are a part of my shoulder-chest holding. With this exercise I begin to organize a space or an inner distance from this on-going physical stance. I begin to disengage from a past that is presently with me. I organize tensions in the neck, head, and shoulders to prevent myself from shrinking and collapse. With the HOW I begin to give myself more room. I begin to form a relationship with myself and others that distinguishes distance from rejection and identifies closeness with adulthood.

> *The goal of the Five Steps is to disorganize the patterns of pain and reorganize contraction into contact, desire to intimacy, aloneness to relationship and community.*

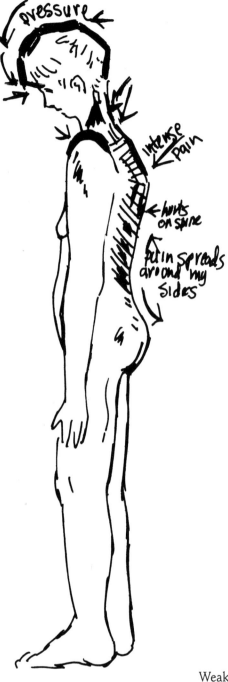

LOUISE

My juicier parts
are unlived under
the power of my
back armor

My back keeps me erect

Weak feeling in vertebrae, neck, spine

Muscles pull back towards spine,
holding in anger, confusion, sadness,
hurt, fear. I fear no identity,
and I fear the aloneness of not being loved.

In my arms and legs I want to throw a tantrum,
but does an abandoned child dare to throw a
tantrum if there is no one to respond?

In my family I had mixed connections to my father and mother. In trying to be close to my father, I became like my brother, a son. I wanted to prove that I was the best son he had, but I was a girl. I learned from my father that I should never have to depend on a man to support me, I should have a good career, make money, manage on my own. From my mother I learned a negative view of sexuality and how to use sexuality to have power over men. I have a female body yet I am terrified of being female.

I am a little *girl* in relationship to my father (Somagram 5). My hands are extended to receive and be received, my face is joyful and playful, but I lack a sense of legs and a belly. In this picture I am about 6 to 8, with a close connection to my father, "I'm special to daddy," "Daddy makes me feel good."

My next somagram (Somagram 6) indicates the confusion between being a *daughter* to my father and in fact, trying to be his *son*. I work in the male world, trying to outdo the other men, to be the best "son," while at the same time I fight my father's fight, getting revenge for what a big corporation did to him, which was to force him into bankruptcy.

My role as *woman* to my father, (Somagram 7). Here I must still female feelings and pelvic excitation. Genital feelings give me shame and guilt. I seek acceptance, "please love me."

I am a *girl* to my mother (Somagram 8). My somatic image is one of fear and confusion with a frozen startle in the eyes. I am a "good girl," cleaning house, being obedient, helping mommy. There is stilled longing in my throat, a splitting off at the waist, a lack of gender, no legs or belly, frozen arms. My lower body is compliant and passive.

I am a *daughter* to my mother (Somagram 9) but totally without gender. My mother's old messages are in me, "being a sexual female is being a whore," "a wife lets her husband humiliate her because she has to once they are married." My face is frozen, jaw like a rock. My eyes are cold and distant. There is fear in my upper chest. I am pulled-up and out of my genitals to protect myself against the world and being invaded. My hands are frozen, much like the arthritic hands of my mother, in a gesture of "don't give, don't take."

The last drawing (Somagram 10) represents the *woman* I want to be in relation to my mother. This is my present image. I am looking to find a body. I want to incorporate qualities of femaleness in my body and in my life. They key image is that of a wolf in my belly, giving me softened strength and the ability to stand on my own two feet. The startled deer reflex which is frozen in the upper part of the body as seen in the previous somagrams, is disorganized.

Using the Five Steps means giving myself a pair of legs as well as a structure which contains me. In disorganizing the frightened little girl, I am beginning to form an adult self.

Girl To My Father:
Hands extended to receive and be received
In the face joyfulness and playfulness
No sense of legs
No belly

Role:
As little girl to my father, make daddy happy
I'm special to daddy, he makes me feel good
Age-up to six or eight

Raised arms in expectation
Wanting a hug
Wanting to be picked up
In later years, wanting acceptance

Legs unsteady, as if learning to walk
Daddy, please catch me if I fall

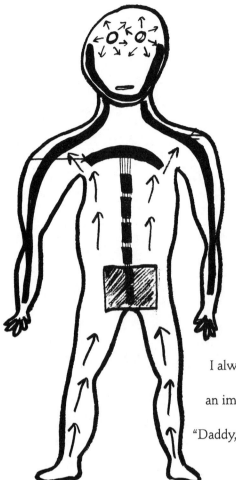

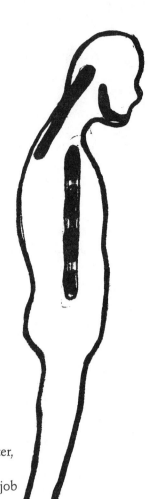

Daughter To My Father:

I always thought of myself as my father's daughter,
yet in drawing this I realize I am his son
an image I lived out right up to the ending of my job
in the male world.
"Daddy, let me prove to you I am better than my brother,
I am your best son."

becomes

Son To My Father:

Role: "I'll fight the world of men for what they
did to my father (a big corporation take-over
resulted in my father's bankruptcy when I was 16).
Role: Martyr, fighter, the armored amazon.

Face: frozen, startle pulled up out of eyes.	Jaws: protruding, stiff, steel, clenched to take what is coming

Eyes braced against world

Chest: constricted band	Shoulders: solid, rigid, freezing against world

Arms: cold, rigid unyielding, ungiving	Legs: ungrounded, pulled up off ground, braced against world

From genitals to band in chest there is freezing, squeezing
Constricted terror, breathing cut off from belly

Woman To My Father:
Gendered feelings and pelvic excitation to be stilled
Any genital feelings bring on shame and guilt
Role: please accept me as I am
please love me

Bands, areas of tightness trying to contain or keep
under control sadness in eyes and face; when these
bands begin to soften, I experience great sadness

Internally I still my longing in my upper
chest and shoulders and cut off my breathing

Tightness/constriction in upper shoulders, leading
into neck and jaw as if I tighten myself to keep
from comforting my father or wanting him to comfort me

Feelings of compassion in my arms
cut off at my hands, the final
stilling of reaching out

Broken energy flow into my legs,
legs ready for flight or collapse,
or become totally rigid to keep rage
in control

Heat/excitation in genitals
I have to keep breathing
to diffuse the excitation and
relax my belly

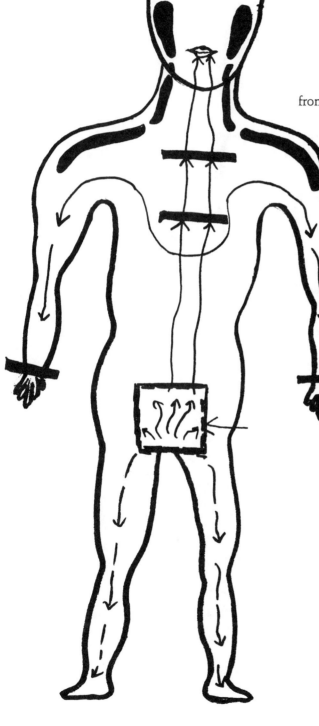

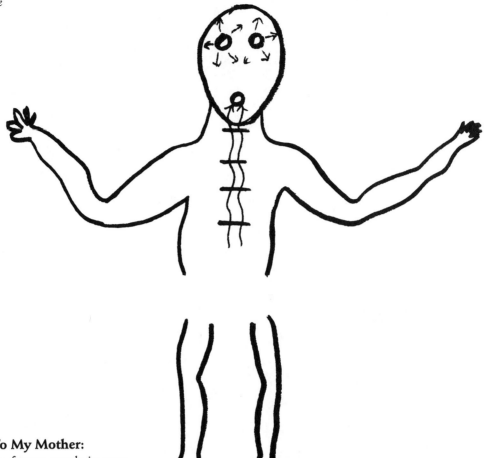

Girl To My Mother:
Fear, confusion, frozen startle in eyes
Stilled, squeezed longing in throat
Split off at waist
No genderedness, no legs, no belly
Frozen arms
Compliant, passive in lower part of body

Role: "I'm a good girl."
What do I have to do to be good?
Performing, cleaning house, helping mommy

Mouth: stiffled longing in mouth and throat
"Don't cry, mommy will be mad if I cry,"

Eyes: clinging to mommy with my eyes
"What is it that you want me to do?"

Hands/arms: Frozen, startle, terror
"Please accept me, please don't hurt me."

Belly: no gendered feeling
Mother's message: genital feelings are bad,
they will be punished

Legs: ready to flee

Daughter To My Mother:
Frozen face, bands of rock across jaws
Steel, distant eyes
Fear in upper chest
Pulled up from genitals to protect myself
Frozen hands
Total denial of genderedness

Eyes: startle, fear, pushing away
"Don't invade me, please love me."

Head: dismembered
breathing cut off by squeezing
of throat and neck

Rage and terror is constricted on the inside,
rage is kept under control by tight squeezing
Externally, a passive, obedient girl but
rage bursts through at the drop of a hat

Hands: Cut off from
"Don't reach out."
"To reach out is to give yourself away."

Legs: Ready for flight
Lack of feeling

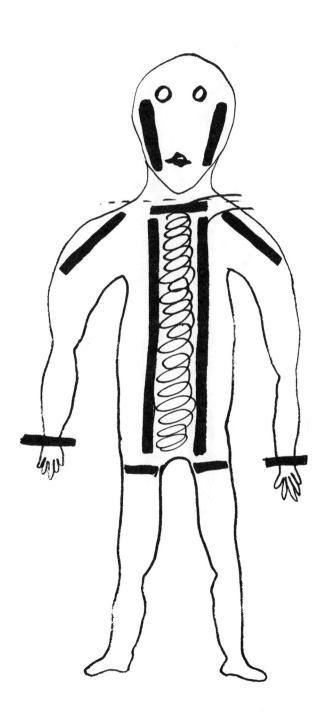

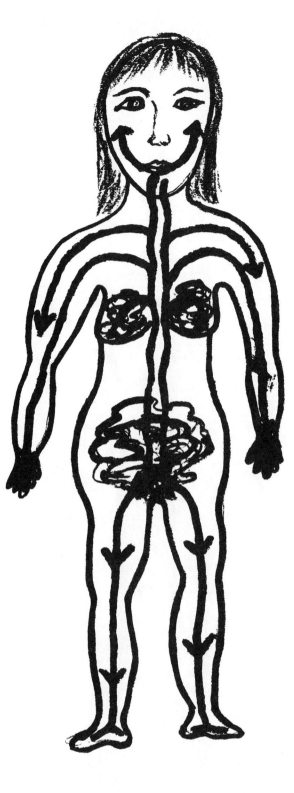

Woman To My Mother:
At present, this is an image looking for a body
The image is that of a wolf in my belly,
giving me softened strength and the ability
to stand on my own two feet
The startled deer reflex is disorganized

Face: heat, warmth, compassion
softened sadness

Arms/hands: ready
to give and to receive,
extend and withdraw

Belly: genital excitation filling my body,
belly round, strength in pulsating, protective
yet gentle, with longing feelings and wanting
to be received

Legs: Firmly on the ground
Connected to pelvis
Able to extend into the world with soft
strength yet also withdraw back into myself

Somagrams help to describe life situations, illuminating the structure that generates and perpetuates a story. We create internal dialogue, make pictures and action patterns, give meaning and feeling to a story which is continued by the symphony of bodily emotional form.

The Five Steps allow exploration of somagrams, to inhibit present actions and rehearse future ones. Step One shows the image of our story, our present situation and form. Step Two indicates how shape and conflicts are maintained. Step Three, the accordion of more and less form, gives the basis of disorganization. With Step Four, there is incubation and creation. Step Five brings a reassertion of our previous form or a new shape to practice.

The HOW steps are a recall of a past organization and rehearsal as well as a way to reorganize ourselves. Stories and somagrams offer the means while the Five Steps provide the tool for forming experience.

form—the past in the present

6

Human growth and development is guided by a powerful set of internal rules which can become distorted by genetic malfunctions and negative parental environments. Negative experiences inhibit or breakdown pump functions, inflaming them or slowing them down. Growth becomes more difficult, self-image deteriorates, we become segmented. Certain functions become exaggerated while others atrophy. The stress of introjected insults weakens the bioexcitatory state and our immune responses. When introjected insults inhibit forming, the result is physical distress, respiratory attacks, locomotion problems, emotional and cognitive distortions. If negative experiences occur in the first few years, inner and outer layers collapse or swell. If negative experiences occur in later years, rigidity and compaction result.

If a parent hounds us to do things a specific way, we introject that experience and become a performer. We seek to please and look to others for direction. If a parent rejects us, we develop an internal image of inadequacy. These interactions with the environment not only interfere with growth and form, they also distort body image, self-perception, and the way we think.

The HOW exercise increases awareness of introjected insults and their accompanying muscular and emotional patterns and restores the integrity of the pump and accordion function of the tubes. This restored pattern of sensation gives rise to a healthy self-image.

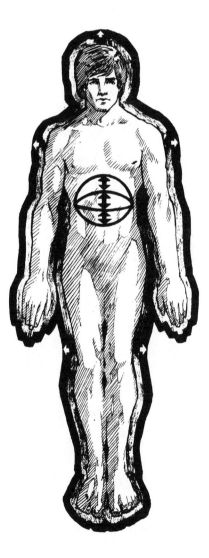

PRESSURING YOURSELF
The Creation of Form

Excitation reflects and sustains the body's shape in a contractile continuum—the accordion function of expansion and contraction. Excitation is cause and result, the messenger as well as the message. It leads to general arousal and then manifests that arousal. Behavior is provoked by excitement and it is excitement. Waves of excitement generate behavior, and when excitement is intense and prolonged, new behavior is produced—being in love, being afraid. New perception and action come into play and learning takes place.

Arousal is a shock, painful or pleasurable. When we experience shock, attention heightens. Responses triggered by memory and past learning change the rate of pulsation, producing attentiveness, increased arousal, and some free-floating excitement. This unfixed excitement is then formed by the brain of the entire organism into a piece of behavior. It is generally recognized that the brain forms excitement into behavior by routing it or calling forth certain past behaviors.

The charged excitatory currents and altered pulsations resulting from shock can be temporary, in which case the organism returns to its regular state. However, increased excitation can become permanent, establishing a chain of reactions which change the architecture of the brain, shape the whole organism and lock into memory.

DIMINISHING SELF TO OVER-EXTENDING SELF

Life offers stimulation and challenges as well as threats and danger. When challenged or faced with continuing danger, we send ourselves an alarm. Alarm increases available excitement, activity, and pulsation. Emotional shock, loud noises, jarring surprises, and physical danger produce a startle reflex. Startle is an instant response that mobilizes a series of reactions along a continuum—stiffening with alertness, rigidifying with fear, bracing with intent to strike, turning away in preparation for flight. To respond, we raise our center of gravity, pull in the abdomen, raise the chest, brace the arm and neck muscles, pull up the genitals, increase respiration. We prepare to act—to push away, turn away, hit, run, or scare the other off. If startle turns into extreme shock, the organism freezes, holds its breath, becomes stiff. If startle continues and we can't run away, we give in, withdraw, collapse, and become helpless.

The startle continuum involves two general responses. In the first, the organism pulls up, braces, readies to attack or turn away. This involves increased organization and calls for more form, more activity, more muscle contraction. This response narrows the organism, increases pressure, and compresses the pulsatory pattern of peristalsis. The second reponse involves decreased organization, a loss of form, disorganization, withdrawal and collapse. There is diminution of pressure, pulsation slows down, muscle and organ tone slacken. If shock is prolonged, the person passes through the rigid phase and enters into a pattern of disorganization with accompanying feelings of despair and helplessness.

The startle response can become a continuous condition, a complex organization from which the organism cannot free itself. The reflexes of expansion and contraction stand at the heart of the startle response. When the reciprocal pattern of expansion and contraction cannot be completed, organizational distress results. The organism becomes fixated in bracing, swelling, compacting, or collapsing. Bracing and compacting are overbound patterns involving more form, organization, and activity. Swelling and collapsing are underbound patterns involving less form, organization, and activity. The startle continuum and its continuation as overbound and underbound structures is the subject of *Emotional Anatomy*.

When these organizations continue for long periods of time, set patterns are established, habitual feelings and functions become embodied on different layers. Families that are repressive or over-protective create children that are underformed prepersonally. Other families over-sexualize their children, demanding a sexual identity before the child is ready. This is an example of being overformed prepersonally. A child could be underformed societally—shy, fearful of others, undersocialized. Alternately, he might be oversocialized—always living out a social role or trying to perfect

INSULTS TO FORM
The Overbound Response

INSULTS TO FORM
The Underbound Response

it. Some are underformed personally, so impressed by nature or social conditioning that they have no stance against these forces. Others, who are overformed, are so in love with their own image that they fail to consider others and end up isolated.

Overbound and underbound startle responses destroy basic identity, innate shape and motility. The HOW process offers a way to disorganize and reorganize distress patterns. The accordion exercise re-establishes the basic pulsations of life, the fundamental patterns of going out and coming back, the excitatory, emotional waves and tides which are the basic language of wholeness.

Elongating, compacting, swelling, and shrinking have an organization, a definite sequence of events. Step One begins with the organization. Step Two involves muscle contraction or elongation, what we actually do to create this shape. Step Three invokes the accordion exercise. When we engage in the accordion exercise, elongation and contraction are exaggerated and made more evident. More tension calls forth the pulling-in reflex, Step Four, detaching us from present action. We precipitate a whole series of organismic contractions, calling out the opposite program, the assertive-elongating process, lengthening-out after pulling-in. The elongation reflex, Step Five, organizes us to re-enter the world in a new way.

How do we pull in? What is our image of it? How do we initiate it? How does it proceed by itself? How do we inhibit it? How do we encourage inhibition to continue? When does it stop? How does it stop? How do we come out of it to organize an assertive reflex? What do we experience as we organize a social role of self-assertion? What do we actually do? What must we inhibit? What do we learn when we are upright, moving towards others?

It is important to have a full range of expansion and contraction, to be able to say yes or no, to give or withhold, to encourage or discourage pulsations, and express emotional currents or contain them. The HOW methodology encourages a fuller range of expansion and contraction and thus reorganizes fixated responses to stress.

THE RESTORATION OF PROCESS

The HOW exercise is emotional re-education—the restoration, encouragement, articulation, and discovery of the ordering or forming process of a person. How does a person speak to himself? What is the language he uses in his internal dialogue? Self-dialogue involves the language of sensation, patterns of organ motility, heightened or lowered excitatory patterns, hormonal flows, and emotional configurations recognized as lusts and passions. These inner dialogues order our existence.

The Five Steps focus on concrete perceptions and actions and ask: "How are you in pain?" or "How are you being angry?", rather than "*What* are you angry about?" How, in fact, do you move a muscle, experience that movement and make that movement? What are the steps you invoke to repress your own natural order and succumb to the demands of society or someone else? The somatic quality of how you do something reveals the nature of your organization. The way you maintain or avoid your own order is found in how you pressure yourself, make yourself flaccid or rigid, become over-active or passive. Personal freedom lies in discovering these somatic patterns.

When a person follows the Five Steps, he makes an interesting discovery. The living, organizing force is often viewed as invisible and unseen, yet, in fact, it is quite concrete and capable of being experienced in the muscular activities of daily existence. This force is the most pervasive and denigrated experience in daily existence despite its being easily observable in the muscular organization accompanying all thinking, acting, and feeling.

The Five Steps help a person know and become intimate with his own order or form. In individual therapy sessions, I may ask a person how he does something, and then expect him to physically and muscularly do it. I want him to experience how he uses himself, for example, how he listens, makes distance from others, engages in self-dialogue. I might ask a person to lie down and bounce on a bed in order to develop a rhythm inside himself. Then, I watch how he maintains that rhythm and the feelings that come with it or how it influences his perception and action. One question I might ask is, "How can you be more or less aggressive?" Or "How do you make tension for yourself?" Slowly, step-by-step, he builds a somatic-emotional language and understands that he is a symphony of movements, not just cognitions and emotions.

Childhood teaches that actions have consequences. Children learn to think before they act and, thereby, conclude that the mind controls the body. But activity is organized. The discovery of how events are ordered, internally and externally, establishes personal truth. This is most significant. At the heart of behavioral disturbances and conflicts, one realizes that he has not organized his own way of doing things.

Somatic process work is not interested in ideals or performances. This is an age of psychological fascism in which true individuality and natural order are distorted. Certain ideals become incorporated: "Thou shalt always improve," "thou shalt always be better," "thou shalt always be smart." Few religions could dream up the many "should's" of the modern world. There are not many ways to discover and live a rhythmic life, a life with its own natural order. The Five Steps deprogram these "should's" and uncover the dynamic organizing force which works in a person to create his own form.

To be formative is to embody, use, shape your experience.

The essence of being human is the ability to interrupt an intended form of behavior and to make another one. Shaping something pertinent to the present is different than being on automatic, a continuation of the past. The mystery of how form is organized and replicated is what the HOW exercise is all about.

Somatic process work establishes the dynamics of how excitement and feeling are organized vertically and in layers, how these dyanmics affect self image and the quest for satisfaction, how shape determines the nature of contact with others, and how work with process restores, affirms, and encourages self-formation. By working with basic assertive and pulling-in patterns, people experience the foundation of life and give themselves a reference by which to judge their existence and growth.

CASE STUDIES

Pleasure and satisfaction, pain and distress are linked emotionally to how we use ourselves. When the organizing process is interfered with, pain results. When we begin to disorganize patterns of exercise and work, love and play, we disorganize ideals. As we disorganize patterns that inhibit excitement or pulsatory uniqueness, we recognize fatigue, muscular confusion, deep aches and pains that were previously ignored. In entering Step Four—the return to basic pulsatory rhythms—we begin to link basic protoplasmic process to societal and personal concepts of performance and have a chance to organize behavior that brings pleasure and satisfaction.

The following case studies, selected from my private practice, describe the problems and pain of certain clients as failures to complete the Five Steps.

ANGELA
BRACING FOR CONTACT AND APPROVAL

Angela is a thirty-year-old woman who, as a child growing up, was blamed for every family crisis. She was constantly told to be more responsible. Her response was to be isolated and distant from her family, while at the same time feeling needy and dependent. She stiffened at every demand, braced herself and said NO. This same bracing also warded off her fear of collapse.

Angela's upper body is stiff and flattened. She complains about rigidity in the neck and head, never letting herself relax, always being on guard. Being in the world involves constant anxiety. On the one hand, she seeks approval from others, yet, on the other, she is always critical. Her stiffness makes her feel small, and also strong.

As she does the Five Steps, making the contractions in her arms, chest, neck, jaw, and eyes more intense, she recognizes that she is constantly rigid with fear—waiting to be psychologically insulted or emotionally abused. Stiffness gives her the appearance of being tough, and alienates her from contact with others. This is Step One, her somatic image.

As we explore how she braces and unbraces, she learns that her self-protecting, isolating contractions are automatic and make her miserable. Harsh voices, angry looks, lack of response—all spell danger and make her tighten up. The normal stance of "I need to know you" gets translated into "I fear to know you, or touch you, or ask for something." When she softens, in Step Three, she experiences vulnerability without reprisal. She experiences a diminution in her physical pain and her emotional isolation. Reorganizing gives her more feeling and self-knowledge, even though both scare her. As she trusts herself and accepts her child-like form, she experiences sensations of lengthening, feelings of expansion, and internal softening. Waves of excitement move through her. Step Four permits Step Five, experiments with new behavior which rebuild her self-identity. She begins to know herself other than as a contracted, isolated girl.

Angela begins to disorganize and reorganize the ways she makes herself small. Now she can push other people away and not deny her need for contact. She learns to give and take from herself and give in to her feelings. Working with her process by herself and with me, she changes her world view. She views being with others as a process of give and take, not brace and ask. She can get tight or loose, feel needy or be strong, push-away or take-in.

ANGELA
Emotional Anatomy
Overbound: Rigid and Dense

Ellen tries to be whatever is necessary. For her, identity is attachment. Formlessness is a ritual. She sees herself as avoiding the demands of materialistic society. Events should happen, she feels, rather than be manipulated or exploited.

Ellen is thirty-five, the daughter of an affluent middle-class family, suffering from uncontrollable rages directed at her child. Her lack of form results in a lack of self-identity. Physically she is short and square. I expected to see a muscular, chunky body but, instead, I found a delicate bone structure, toneless muscles, and little propensity for quick muscular action. She is like putty. She appears affectless, unbounded and needs others to define her, to give her limitations, to offer resistance. During the course of our work she chides me for not setting up boundaries for her.

She dislikes conflict. This feeling creates emotional confusion for her. She explodes whenever her child makes demands or holds his ground, something she is unable to do. When she does not get her way, she becomes violent or deprecating. She wants others to give her boundaries. She has deep but unrecognized feelings of wanting to be filled up or given form.

Ellen has no form, she fears yet longs for it. She destructures every build-up of form with explosiveness or with harmonizing incorporation. She lives in Steps Three and Four. Her global excitement and uncontrolled emotions reveal a woman at the mercy of impulses, unable to inhibit herself to make boundaries.

Her lack of form does not sustain excitement or give her a sense of being full or satisfied. She associates being wanted with being used. Her body is a tidal pool where life is undifferentiated and primitive. She has no hope of sustaining a form which would make her self-managing.

I encourage her to practice the accordion exercise over and over so that she can gain the experience of using her muscles to give a sense of form and self-containment. It is important for her to form her own boundaries, so that she can tame the energetic excesses of her infantile self.

It is my task with Ellen to expose what is unformed in her, using Step One and Two, the deep power of her organizing urges, to give boundaries or contain the events of daily existence. Her experience of developing sustained rhythmical patterns brings a sense of self-worth, and self-management.

Creating form is not easy. It takes commitment and willingness to struggle, especially if one has been overprotected. Resistance and obstacles give form and are learned early in life. Forming the unformed differs from forming what has once been lived into a fresh shape.

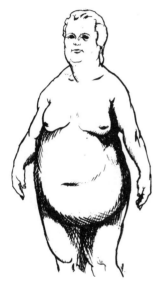

ELLEN
Emotional Anatomy
Underbound: Swollen

Larry keeps himself continually occupied in order to avoid being noticed. His specialty is avoiding demands. He sees himself as small, insignificant with no useful function. He does as little as possible. Forming anything is not even a dream. Larry lives in Step Two—performing by rote what is minimally expected. He uses himself cautiously, fearfully, with self-deprecation.

Larry is a dense, rigid person who has been humiliated into becoming small. He is overbound, his thorax collapsed from the muscle spasms around his chest, neck, and shoulders. Larry is secretive and silent, his facial expression a grim mask. The muscles of his jaw and cheeks are like bands of steel. This compressed pattern is his basic self-organization.

Larry avoids rejection and seeks approval. Every life situation is a potential rejection, an opportunity to feel worthless. He emits a constant silent plea for approval. Larry needs immediate acceptance. Without it, he retreats by pulling in his chest. Pulling-in is his basic organization. In talking with him, I find that his fear comes from his early years where nothing he did at home was adequate or satisfactory. He became fearful and shy and formed a personality of lowered expectations, or anticipated rejection for every effort.

The ridicule that Larry suffered is responsible for the powerful muscle constrictions in his compressed chest. He inhibits his own arousal and organizes low self-esteem. He organizes himself to be inconspicuous. To maintain this stance he needs to hold himself in and then quickly expel whatever struggles to emerge. He is uncaring. Sexually, his pattern is the same, giving him feelings of impotence and undermining his maleness. Since he sees the world as hostile and unaccepting and himself as inadequate, he structures the reflex patterns of fear and inhibition into a permanent form. There is no way that Larry can go through the steps of self-forming alone.

Larry holds down his impulses and then violently releases them on specific occasions. Through the accordion exercise, Larry learns to unstructure his inhibitions. The upwelling of his visceral urges helps him grow a personal space by expanding his chest, internal organs, and brain.

By undoing Steps One and Two, the image of defeat and the muscular attitude of compression, Larry is able to destructure fear, incubate enthusiasm, and utilize the resulting excitation to practice a new form. Through expansion, he softens his skeletal-muscular inhibitions. I help him with exercises that provide a sense of rhythmicity. He experiences

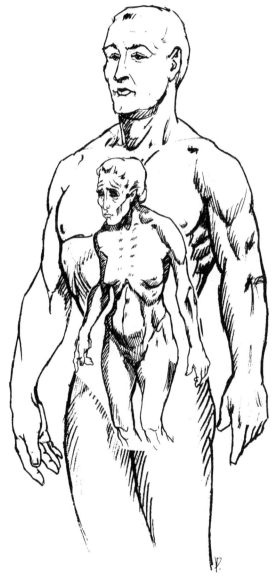

LARRY
Emotional Anatomy
Outer-Rigid
Inner-Collapsed

waves of pulsation, develops an inner dimension, and discovers that pressure from inside is asserted outward instead of against himself. Steps Three and Four permit an inner swelling and tidal action and the practice of Step Five gives him a chance to use himself assertively, keeping his space and rhythmicity going. Descending out of this rigidity, Larry finds an internal set of pulsations that enhance his arousal. This helps him develop a new sense of self and connection to others. His sense of maleness and self-assertion grows.

MARY
AN ADULTIFIED CHILD

Mary imagines herself the perfect wife. She appears sexy, sophisticated, cheerful, provocative and amusing. She knows how to get attention from men and how to make her husband find her desirable. To perpetuate her somatic image, she makes her life a continuous performance, acting out images of what she should be rather than what she feels.

While externally she performs as Mrs. Perfect Young Woman, underneath she is timid, pulled-in, plagued with dissatisfactions. Mary, the sex goddess, is really a child, passive and confused, acting out societal images of femininity. Taking cues from others, she performs the recommended rituals of behavior.

Her pattern of holding-back gives her a rigid, defiant, muscle-bound look. Her chest is lifted and thrust out, her arms held smartly and stiffly at her sides. Her pelvis lacks spontaneous feeling, only diminished sensations. Her excitement is in intense and seemingly endless fantasies. Her sexual movements are mechanical and performance-oriented. She yearns to reach beyond the anxieties of her roles, but fears her husband's rejection. She feels cheated and resentful. Despite her use of the symbols of sexuality, she is not a sexual, feeling person but a slave to images and ideals.

Mary lives in Steps One and Two, image and performance. Her excitation is a closed circuit between fantasy and sexual performance. Since there are no tides of excitement to generate feeling, she has no inner emotional form and suffers terribly from feelings of inadequacy. She wards off negative feelings with muscular rigidities and more social performance.

Working with Mary involves using the HOW methodology in a number of areas of her life. How does she make herself a child by contracting her pelvis? How does she make herself bigger than she is by lifting her chest? How does she imagine these roles, actually make them, and take them

MARY
Emotional Anatomy
Outer-Dense
Inner-Swollen

down? How does she ground herself first in performance and ideals and then in her own internal process? How does she make herself bigger by living in her fantasies?

For Mary to make a new form, it is essential to end her role as performer. When she destructures her performer, she allows her own images to emerge. She creates self-esteem by removing the gross discrepancy between her public life as sex object and her private life as child-like. As she destructures her lifted chest and rigid pelvis, she descends into her true ground.

With Steps Three and Four, Mary begins to inhibit her performer and connect to her visceral life. Settling into Step Four, insights are linked to new feelings and organ sensations. By being inside herself, she uses Steps Two and Five to assert her own way of being a woman.

7 *the formative journey*

THERE is no experience without embodiment. There is no embodiment without experience, no existence without a body. Because I am embodied, I exist.

Human anatomy and behavior have order and organization. We see this in embryology from the command to replicate to the different stages that create a human. We see this in the various bodies that comprise a personal history, specialized shapes progressing from youth to old age. This progression is a journey marked by order and organization.

Sociological and personal shaping follow a similar pattern of organization. This pattern is innate, it is there as inherited tradition. We live this pattern in an unconscious way as part of nature and society. It is our destiny. There is an order and an organization from which to create a personal life. I call this formativeness.

To be true to yourself means identifying with this ongoing process of formativeness. We call this individuating, self-actualizing, fulfilling your potential, or being yourself. Without a commitment to your own process, you must trust someone else's vision of who you should be and how to get there.

Every organism has a unique way of organizing itself. Through a continuing dialogue between the urge to individuate and the urges of society and nature, a person develops. Through this interaction a form is created, one that reflects the truth of the prepersonal, personal, and postpersonal layers. The goal of therapy thus becomes how we form ourselves, how we organize and disorganize experience. This is different than insight, individuation, increased excitation, or the integration of dissociated experiences. Therapy reinstitutes the formative process as the baseline of experience by which we form ourselves and a life.

> *The formative journey is to know our secret depths through a process that transforms us from animal to human.*

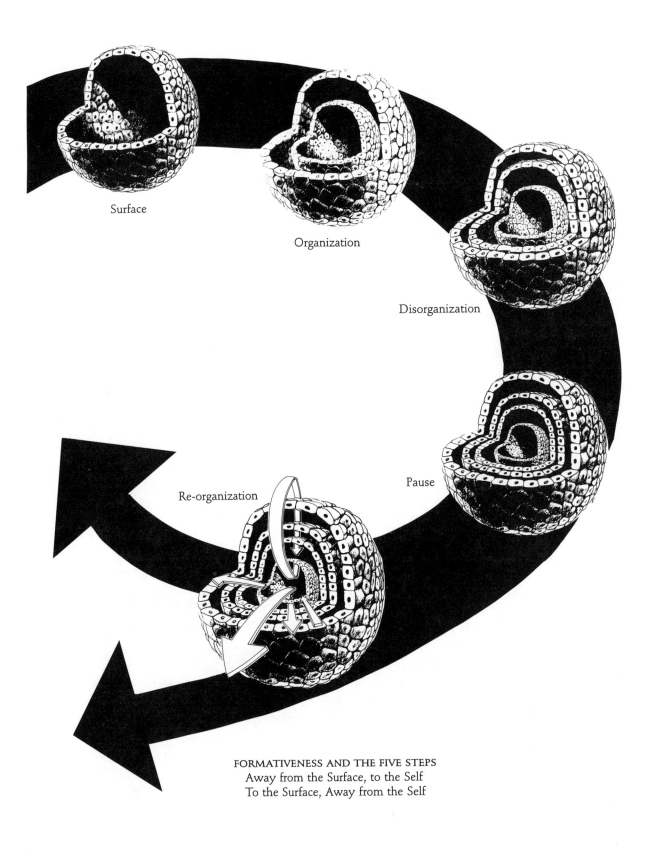

Surface

Organization

Disorganization

Pause

Re-organization

FORMATIVENESS AND THE FIVE STEPS
Away from the Surface, to the Self
To the Surface, Away from the Self

The journey has a beginning and an end. It is a chain of living events organized in such a way that it forms a continuum, an on-going life, a living shape. The concretization of any of our experiences along this continuum is the somatic self. This somatizing is both a universal as well as a personal experience. It is body on its way to becoming another body. Generated by this process are excitation, feelings of challenge, fears that we may not make it, as well as the emotions of rejection and affirmation of our early familiar life. This is an embryological-like pattern, the formative pattern of order and organization in operation.

We think of ourselves as having one shape or somatic configuration. But, in fact, we are a series of shapes, a perpetual organization of infant, child, adolescent, adult. This is the tale of all change. We are not the same body self as we were five, ten, twenty years ago. We suffer when we resist the process of cellular and psychological transformation. Illness is accompanied by the resistance to or ignorance about how to form and reform. When we insist on always being the same, we deform ourselves. When we push, exaggerate, and inflate our capacities, we deform ourselves. Much human misery results from not being part of the journey of unforming and reforming.

The most important aspect of the formative journey is the ability to embody experience. When experience is embodied passively, the great unconscious controls shape, but a personal form develops when experience is used and digested. As experience becomes embodied, shape differentiates into layers, forming an interior or exterior space, organizing psycho-emotional space.

This journey is usually associated with being separate and alone. But is individuality concerned only with separation, differentiation, being alienated? Our emotional experience confirms this yet our behavior seeks connection, contact, community, relationship. We know ourself by the spikes of desire that reach for connection, contact, and shaping. Our movement through the personal journey of our life, whether we know it or not, communicates experience to the great sea of others around us about how we live. Embodying our lived experience is participating in and contributing to the struggle of the general community to reach its form.

An analysis of our environmental upbringing reveals that we all live in an adrenalized state. The dialogue between the brain and the rest of the body is a reciprocal and oscillating pattern in which aliveness is equated with increased excitation. That is the generalized state of our consciousness, what we equate with wisdom, knowledge, and consciousness. But what happens if you break that chain, disorganize the localization of excitation and induce a generalized rather than a specific state? That is the function of the Five Steps.

The Five Steps help you know and feel how your present state is organized, how excitement and emotion become personal and give rise to the urge to form yourself as your experience deepens.

The somatic-emotional exercises contained throughout the book demonstrate how the focus of excitation may be changed. The Five Steps both reveal and create a state. They do not drive you to more excitement or feeling or bring you anywhere; rather they interfere with the organization that stands between you and your basic mechanism. They simply reveal what is there. The challenge is, what do you do with this information after you receive it?

The organism is more plastic than we realize. It is not hard-wired totally. New organization can occur. Nature has devised a way to make corrections. That is what human biology is all about. That is what personal somatic process is all about and what the Five Steps and somatic-emotional exercise reveal. The Steps ask, how are you going to use the functions that you have to organize or disorganize a particular attitude to yourself or another? Or are you going to perpetuate a past attitude? In organizing and disorganizing you have the possibility of creating another type of relationship to yourself or another.

The steps of the formative process are more than a self-help tool or a psycho-somatic technique for self-improvement. They are a reference for living which restore a sense of organismic-emotional truth, grace and beauty. The Five Steps are a means for embodying or forming experience into a living design that speaks our truth, encourages our own cellular life and a growing intimacy with how we live.

What is formed in us is often in conflict with what is unformed, or what must be reformed. Maintaining organizations that we have inherited or created can clash with disorganizing forms that no longer serve us, and organizing forms where none have existed before.

We construct a self by organizing events out of prepersonal and postpersonal experiences. We are given a body by nature and challenged to live it. We are initiated into a societal shape and commanded to live it. But the formed or personal self is not a given, it needs encouragement to form.

The intensification and de-intensification of Steps Two and Three show how an internal personal layer is organized. The forming self can be visualized as a growing child. A child moves from an unformed potential to a formed adult. He embodies his experiences into a personal "I," and makes them a personal possession. In organizing a self, he acquires an identity, a somatic image going by a name.

Each of us may find one or another of the steps attractive while we neglect others. There are people who are attracted to Step Two—action, organization, structure. The hero image, challenge, danger—all are symbols of this state. Yet others shy away from action or organization because it frightens them. Others identify with Step Three, symbols of taking apart, tearing down, fragmentation. But the state of disorganization may fill others with dread, anxiety which

> *The Five Steps organize contact and separation, taking and giving, love and distance, and help you make your life.*

they try to avoid. Some seek Step Four—passivity, receptivity, going with the flow, chaos. Others prefer formality and structure. Finally, there are those attracted to Step Five, seeking the messiah, looking for causes to change things while others prefer things as they are.

This book is about life as a formative process. We form first by the command of nature, then by society, then by a personal struggle to form volitionally our experience. The images and self-reflection exercises throughout this book depict this. They show the current of life, the form of destiny, and a way to work with the Five Steps to grasp how we function and create order and form.

We have a given self and a formed, lived self, we intensify and de-intensify all our mental, emotional, organic functions. We are always collating our experiences and organizing them into an ongoing story with instinctual elements. There are mythic themes, the organic life of the world organism; societal themes, acts as part of the social mission, and the personal drama of the hero's journey, transforming ourselves through the different stages of our life.

The urge to create a personal form is as vital as the reproductive urge. The reproductive urge is an imperative to embody genetic experience into forms that are perpetuated. But internally we also seek to perpetuate our identity, individuality, and humanness.

The formative process is one that unfolds and one that is lived volitionally as best one can. The height of human personal drama is to live this formative process, act it, form it, be lived by it. Hopefully, the formative process is then grasped as our personal life. The Five Steps are ways to identify where and how we can work with ourself to cooperate with our natural process and societal form. We then can appreciate what it means to form a self, prepersonally, societally, personally.

All of us seek connection to the deeper feelings that give life meaning and value. Somatic process reveals the transcendent, a cellular existence organizes anatomy into an emotional, lived truth. We go from passion and desire to union and devotion, from an instinctual order to a social order, from a personal order to the divine. We, as living beings, manifest the mysteries of being human. We generate experiences and organize them into temporal configurations, the geometry by which the human, the personal, the universal is revealed.